# INNOVATIVE WATER FINANCE IN AFRICA

A Guide for Water Managers

## VOLUME 1

## Water Finance Innovations in Context

Edited by
Atakilte Beyene and Cush Ngonzo Luwesi

NORDISKA AFRIKAINSITUTET
The Nordic Africa Institute

UPPSALA 2018

INDEXING TERMS:

Water resources
Water management
Water supply
Sanitation services
Resources development
Financing
Community participation
Africa

Innovative Water Finance in Africa: A Guide for Water Managers
Volume 1: Water Finance Innovations in Context

Edited by Atakilte Beyene and Cush Ngonzo Luwesi

ISBN 978-91-7106-815-6    print-on-demand version
ISBN 978-91-7106-816-3    pdf e-book
ISBN 978-91-7106-817-0    epub e-book

© 2018 The authors and the Nordic Africa Institute

Layout: Henrik Alfredsson, The Nordic Africa Institute

Print on demand: Lightning Source UK Ltd.

Front cover: Nsongwe Village, Zambia, photo credit Brett Kotelko
Back cover: Hands washing. Photo credit Sande Murunga, CIFOR

THE NORDIC AFRICA INSTITUTE (Nordiska Afrikainstitutet) is a centre for
research, knowledge, policy advice and information on Africa. Based in
Uppsala, Sweden, we are a government agency, funded jointly by Sweden,
Finland and Iceland.

The opinions expressed in this volume are those of the author and
do not necessarily reflect the views of the Nordic Africa Institute.

This work is freely available in open access, you can download it online via the
NAI web site, www.nai.uu.se, where you can also purchase print edition copies.

# Contents

# Authors Biographies

**Dr. Atakilte Beyene** is a senior researcher at the Nordic Africa Institute. He holds a PhD from the Swedish University of Agricultural Sciences and has worked in universities and research institutes in Sweden and Ethiopia. His research focuses on agrarian and rural institutions, natural resource management, food security and gender studies. He has conducted extensive field studies in Ethiopia and Tanzania. He has both coordinated and worked on interdisciplinary research projects in Nordic and African countries. His current research includes large-scale agricultural and irrigation investments in Africa, and their implications for local economies.

**Prof. Cush Ngonzo Luwesi** is currently a guest researcher at the Nordic Africa I nstitute (NAI) of the University of Uppsala, Sweden, and a member of the scientific advisory committee of the Climate Research for Development (CR4D) program championed by the United Nations' Economic Commission for Africa (UNECA). He is also an associate professor of economics and environment at the University of Kwango (DR Congo), the Deputy Director General (Academic) at the Health College of Kenge (DR Congo). Prior to these assignments, he was the Focal Region Manager of the CGIAR Research Program on Water, Land and Ecosystems (WLE) in West Africa, a program managed by the International Water Management Institute (IWMI) on behalf of the Consultative Group for International Agriculture Research (CGIAR). He attained PhD, Msc and MA degrees in economics of water and climate change from Kenyatta University (Nairobi) and the University of Kinshasa (DR Congo).

**Dr. Joy Apiyo Obando** is an Associate Professor at the Department of Geography, Kenyatta University specializing in Physical Geography, Geomorphology and Integrated Watershed Management. She works as an interface between physical geography and management in the watershed. She coordinated the IWM programme at the Geography Department. Currently her research focuses on groundwater dynamics and watershed management. She coordinates an international Masters programme hosted at Kenyatta University. She has won several national and international research grant awards and has published widely. She is a member of the steering Committee of the International Geographical Union Geomorphology and Society Commission; and also a member of the International Advisory Board of Water Resources Research Center.

**Prof. Raphael Muamba Tshimanga** is a professional of water resources with a PhD degree in hydrology. He currently holds a position of Associate Professor and is the head of the Department of Natural Resources Management at the Faculty of Agronomic Sciences of the University of Kinshasa. He is the regional coordinator of the Congo Basin Network for Research and Capacity Building in Water Resources

(CB-HYDRONET), an affiliate member of a global network for capacity development in water resources (Cap-Net UNDP). The focus of his activities for about past ten years has been on exploring ways for practical implementation of approaches to water resources assessment, management and development. This encompasses areas such as hydrological modelling, water resources assessment and hydrological uncertainty analysis; water resources systems analysis and river basin development; land use and climate change impacts on water resources; application of earth observation information in water resources management; environmental water requirements; Integrated Water Resources Management (IWRM) including water allocation and demand management, institutional and legal framework; capacity building and training in water resources; water resources project evaluation and management.

**Dr. Mamudu Abunga Akudugu** holds a PhD in Livelihoods (International and Rural Development) from the University of Reading, United Kingdom; Master of Philosophy (MPhil) in Agricultural Economics from the University of Ghana, Ghana; and Bachelor of Science (BSc) in Agriculture Technology (Agricultural Economics and Extension Option) from the University for Development Studies, Tamale – Ghana. Dr. Akudugu is currently a Senior Research Fellow at the Institute for Interdisciplinary Research and Consultancy Services (IIRaCS) of the University for Development Studies (UDS) and head of the University Consultancy Services Unit. He has several years of experience in conducting interdisciplinary research, largely employing mixed methods (qualitative and quantitative approaches) in his research activities. He has served as a consultant to many national and international organisations, including the Food and Agriculture Organization of the United Nations. Dr. Akudugu is an active member of the African Association of Agricultural Economists (AAAE) and other professional bodies. His current research focuses on irrigation and rural livelihoods development, climate change and agrarian change, and gender and generational dynamics of development. He has over 20 peer-reviewed publications and has presented papers at many local and international conferences.

**Dr. Linnet Hamasi Henry** is currently a guest researcher at the Nordic Africa Institute (NAI) of the University of Uppsala, Sweden. She is also a lecturer of Conflict, Peace and Strategic Studies at Kenyatta University, Nairobi, Kenya. Previously, she was also a lecturer of history, gender, peace and conflict at Kisii University, Kenya, where she headed the examination office. She also served as the Kenyan Deputy President's Chief of Staff (2013-2014). Dr. Hamasi Henry attained PhD of Arts from Masinde Muliro University of Science and Technology, Kenya. She has widely published, attended and organized many international conferences in the context of the African Interdisciplinary Studies Association (AISA) and the Center for Democracy Research and Development (CEDRED) as well as affiliated universities in Kenya, where she serves as a board member. She had again served as the editorial assistant of the East African Journal of Humanities and Social Sciences (EAJHS). Dr. Linnet Hamasi had also been the project coordinator and the administrator of the research department as well as part-time lecturer of research methods at the Catholic University of Eastern Africa (CUEA).

**Dr. Peter Philip Wambua** is a lecturer of Human Resource Management at the Department of Human Resource Management of Kenyatta University with a best teaching award in 2014. He is accredited with a significant number of publications focusing on performance contracting of teaching academic staffers service delivery and curriculum development in public universities in Kenya using a business perspective. Dr Philip Wambua gives back to the community by sitting and making decisions courtesy of a ministerial appointment in a board of management of Kangundo High School. He is also the manager of a Non-Governmental Organization in Kenya (Zero to One Mission NGO) whose ultimate mission and vision is to uplift the living and educational standards of the disadvantaged in the community.

**Dr. Florence Muthoni Mainah** is a Lecturer of Gender and Development Studies at Kenyatta University, Nairobi, Kenya. She attained PhD and MA of Education at Kenyatta University and the University of Nairobi (Kenya), respectively, with specialization in counseling psychology, gender and development studies. She has extensively published in the areas of assertive training, cognitive restructuring, problem solving skills, communication skills, conflict resolution and anger management for both group and individual therapy. Dr. Mainah has genuine interest in youth and family affairs, and assists in offering psychosocial skills. She is widely consulted by international organizations, including the UNICEF, the Center for International Training and Executive Development (CITE), and the Association of African Universities (AAU). She also volunteers to assist in debriefing internally displaced people (IDPs) on trauma management in the context of Mukuru Economic Empowerment Project (MEEP) and Support for Women in Extreme Difficulties (SWED). She is a counselor at ST. Michael's counseling center, Nairobi and a member of Kenya Counseling Association. Finally, Dr. Manah likes games and swimming, baking, cycling and traveling, collecting rocks and bird watching.

**Dr. Mathabo Khau** holds a PhD in Gender and Education from the University of KwaZulu-Natal, South Africa. As an exchange student at McGill University, Canada, funded through DFAIT in 2007, she offered a number of seminars on sexuality and memory at McGill and Concordia Universities. She has been a postdoctoral fellow in 2010 at Linköping and Örebro Universities' Centre of Gender Excellence in Sweden (Gendering Excellence (GEXcel): Towards a European Centre of Excellence in Transnational and Transdisciplinary Studies of Changing Gender Relations, Intersectionalities and Embodiment). She has also been a postdoctoral fellow at the Nelson Mandela Metropolitan University under the HIV&AIDS Research in Education Chair for 2 years 2011/12. She is a Senior Lecturer in the School of Educational Research and Engagement at the Nelson Mandela Metropolitan University, where she is also the Director for the Action Research Unit, and Head of Department for Postgraduate Studies. Currently she is a Guest Researcher at the Nordic Africa Institute in Uppsala, Sweden. Her research interests are in sexualities, sexual health and reproductive rights, sexual pleasure, gender and curriculum, and HIV in education. She has published several articles in well recognized journals such as Agenda; Sexualities; and Girlhood Studies; and has presented her work at several international conferences.

**Eng. Wangai Ndirangu** is the Principal Engineer of Batiment Engineering and Associates (Beassociates) consultancy service since 2002 and Lecturer at Jomo Kenyatta University of Agriculture and Technology (JKUAT) in Kenya. He graduated from Moi University with a Masters of Philosophy in Water Engineering, and a registered Consultant Engineer by Engineers Registration Board of Kenya. He is also a Member Institution of Engineers of Kenya. He has 20 years postgraduate experience in water, wastewater, project and institutional management support, infrastructural works (structures, roadwork's, landscaping and drainage, standard estates services), and Irrigation. He values human achievement through competence, innovation and mutual learning experience. Hence, he spearheaded the creation of the WaterCap to enable East African professionals to network with other members of the global network for capacity development in water resources (Cap-Net UNDP), to bring a clear understanding of the concept of Integrated Water Resources Management (IWRM) and management expertise to professionals in water management and service delivery from both the proponent's and the experience perspectives.

**Ms. Nele Förch** is a German advisor for institutional development, water governance and integrated water resources management in Eastern Africa, with more than ten years experience. She was the regional coordinator for the Centre for International Capacity Development for the University of Siegen. She is currently a technical advisor with the GIZ Water Sector Reform Programme (WSRP) in Kenya and directly works with the Kenyan Water Resources Management Authority. Her research interests include issues in water governance and integrated watershed management relating to water security, stewardship, participatory processes and particularly conflict transformation.

**Ms. Pauline Matu Mureithi** is a Kenyan consultant in law and environment, with over 30 years of professional experience in the operational legal regime of her country, the region and globally – MEAs. Pauline has a rich career as a senior state attorney, executive chairperson of the environmental ombudsman in Kenya, corporation secretary/head of secretariat for a multinational company (Caltex Oil) and investigator cum trial coordinator for the UN-ICTR, among others. She is currently operating her own Consultancy firm, Lex Consult, while also serving Oxfam International as a Project Lead consultant. Pauline is the proud mother of two grow-up daughters. She was assisted in the legal research and editing by a young, brilliant lawyer named Jacob Malelu.

**Mr. Amos Yesutanbul Nkpeebo** is a project leader with substantive management accomplishments in environmental governance, research socio-technical solutions in Ghana, Cameroon, Cote d'Ivoire and Kenya. Collaborated with leading policy directors to establish capacity building and development activities including Integrated Watershed Management, FLEGT/VPA and REDD+ implementation. Committed to innovative cooperation in climate adaptation, water-land-energy security, forest landscape restoration, climate smart agriculture, and ecosystem valuation. He holds MSc. in Integrated Watershed Management (Kenyatta University, Kenya), BSc. Development Planning (KNUST, Ghana), and Certificate in Professional Project Management (GIMPA, Ghana). Amos currently works with Friends of the Earth-Ghana as the Coordinator for the Programme on Climate Justice and Energy where he advocates for SDG readiness in Sub-Saharan Africa through bio-regional approaches, adaptation data sharing and climate finance-readiness.

**Ms. Elsie Odonkor** is a gender specialist in Ghana. She holds a Master of Philosophy (MPhil) in Development Studies from the University of Development Studies, Ghana and a Bachelor of Arts (BA) in French and Philosophy from the University of Ghana. Elsie is currently a Research Officer (Gender) at the International Water Management Institute (IWMI), West Africa Office, Ghana. Over the years, her research and work focus has focused on agricultural research, water management and social protection. Prior to her work at IWMI, she worked with a team of colleagues at the African Development Programme (ADP) consulted by the UN FAO.

**Ms. Mary N. Mutiso** is the head of The Department of Geography at South Eastern Kenya University (SEKU). She also coordinates the School Of Humanities programs in two of south Eastern Kenya University Campuses. She holds a Bachelor's degree in education and a Master's degree in Urban and regional planning with a bias towards development studies and Economic geography. Mary is a seasoned educator who served as a Deputy Director of Student affairs in Kenyatta University before moving to South Eastern Kenya University. She has over 25 years' experience in teaching and research. Her research interests include development, Natural Resource Management and political ecology. Her current research deals with the Poverty-Environmental Degradation nexus and Eco-Friendly Dry-Land Agriculture and Water Technologies. She is also a devoted discussant on the geo-engineering initiative by Harvard University (US) and German universities.

**Mr. Albert Ruhakana** (Msc) is a researcher at the Department of Natural Resource Management, of the Rwanda Agriculture Board, where he coordinates soil and water management projects. He holds degree in Integrated Watershed Management with substantial post graduate credentials in advanced technologies, GIS and remote sensing applied to watershed management.

**Ms. Aseye Afi Nutsukpui** is a corporate director at Guinness International – West and Central Africa office (Ghana) – where she is in charge of public policy and regulatory affairs. Prior to this appointment, she was the principal communications officer at Stratcomm Africa (Ghana). She is a Master candidate in communications from the University of Ghana, Legon. She holds Bachelor's degree in English and Linguistics from the same university, and is currently pursuing Law studies therein. Ms. Nutsukpui has over 12 years of experience in the communications field in Ghana. As communications professional, mainly working with PR agency, she has delivered communication solutions for institutions in the media, real estate, energy, oil and gas, engineering and construction, sanitation and public services. Her most recent achievement is the development of an Engagement and Communication Plan (ECP) for the International Water Management Institute (IWMI) on behalf of the Consultative Group for International Agricultural Research (CGIAR), specifically the Water, Land and Ecosystems (WLE) programme in the Volta and Niger Basins. Her expertise covers stakeholder and community relations, corporate communication and reputation management, media relations and crisis management among others.

# Preface and Acknowledgements

Water has become increasingly central to addressing multiple development and environmental objectives in the course of climate change. Exploring the multiple dimensions of water governance, policy and management in a holistic way is thus imperative for financial innovations to take place in the water sector. This book on "Innovative Water Finance in Africa" constitutes, first of all, a reference document allowing African managers and policy-makers to broaden their knowledge of financing strategies and tactics in order to raise fund for water services provision and water resources development. But we also hope that global managers and policy-makers will take advantage of this book to review their agenda on water and sanitation services in order to give water resources development a place in their funding structures.

The book will present and discuss the context in which contemporary instruments of financing water services provision and water resources development are emerging in Africa. In this regard, three major thematic areas are recognized as key: (i) A coverage of the legal and institutional contexts pertaining to water financing innovations; (ii) An assessment of economic mechanisms and principles subtending financial innovations in the water sector; and (iii) A sample of cases of applications of innovative water financing mechanisms based on scale formation and adoption practices. Volume I addresses at depth the first thematic area by highlighting the legal, institutional and market contexts in which innovative economic mechanisms and financial schemes are taking place in Africa.

Chapter One is a prologue to the book content focusing on the question "Why does Africa need innovative water financing mechanisms?" The chapter creates awareness on key water issues currently facing Africa and their projected escalation in the near future. It recommends total overhaul of the water sector to introduce participatory management of water resources and of the delivery of water and sanitation services across the continent so that financial innovations can take place. Chapter Two entitled "Africa's water sector development and financing outlook" surveys the various water uses for agriculture and other human activities as well as their related investments in human capital, infrastructure, and research and extension works. It finally answer the question "is financing agricultural water development in Africa a mere dream?" to give not only hope but also evidence and feasible pathways for water developers to believe in an African "green water revolution". Chapter Three introduces the various understandings of the concept of "Integrated Water Resources Management (IWRM)" with a focus on "water governance performance" as its core business. It comes out with clear Intermediate Development Outcomes (IDOs) that would lead to water sector reforms and later to financial innovations. Chapter Four focuses on the cases of the Kenyan water sector reforms of 2002 and 2016 to give an idea of legal, institutional and market requirements for financial innovation to take place. Chapter Five brings marketing in the fundraising system of water companies and institutions to keep finances flowing to the sector through innovative engagement and communication with customers and financiers, financial planning and ring-fencing of water sector revenues supported by good governance, organizational competence and budgetary discipline. Lastly Chapter Six is entitled "'Gender in water finance': A gendered finance perspectives for a paradigm shift in water finance management". It employs some common African saying that look at innovative roles that women can play in securing sustainable water financing in the continent. These include adages such as 'Women do not leave anything to chance' (Strategic management), 'Women talk a lot' (communication and engagement ability), 'Women buy and sell everything they find on their way' (Sales and marketing ability), 'Women are afraid of money' (treasury safeguarding ability).

Of course, this is a book of essays drawn from scholarly works and a workshop that was facilitated by most of the authors in November 2011 in Mombasa, Kenya, which was organized by the Bavarian School of Finance (BfZ, SWAP project) and the Network for Capacity Building in Integrated Water Resources Management in East Africa (WaterCap) in partnership with Kenya Water Institute (KEWI) and Strathmore University. Hence, the book does not, by any means, pretend to replace practice based on country policies and local realities. As the reader goes through the book, he or she realizes that most of the contributions come from East and West Africa, basically from Kenya and Ghana, and to some extent, from Ethiopia, Mali and Lesotho. We believe the book has important contribution for the current scholarly discussion on financial innovations in the water sector of Africa.

We would like to acknowledge the generous support of the Nordic Africa Institute in financing the publication of this book and its staff at Communications Unit for their attentiveness during the editorial works. We thank Mr. Henrik Alfredsson for his professional inputs in the design, layout and indexing of the book.

Uppsala and Kenge, February 2018

*Atakilte Beyene and Cush Ngonzo Luwesi*

# 1. Why Does Africa Need Innovative Water Financing Mechanisms?

Kenya, November 2011. Diarrheal disease is responsible for nearly 1 million deaths per year among children under 5. Use of chlorine keeps water purified for a minimum of 24 hours. The Dispensers for Safe Water (DSW) program provided millions of people with access to chlorine dispensers over three years. Photo credit Jonathan Kalan.

Water is the cause of about 20 deaths in every 100 among the under-5s.

# Some facts about water

Source: The Water Project, 2016

- 1 in 9 people, or 783 million, worldwide do not have access to clean and safe water.[1]
- 84 percent of the people who don't have access to improved water, live in rural areas.[1]
- Girls under the age of 15 are twice as likely as boys to be the family member responsible for fetching water. [1]
- Almost two-thirds of households rely on women to get the family's water when there is no water source in the home. [1]
- 159 million people worldwide still use surface water. Two thirds, or 102 million, of them live in Sub-Saharan Africa.[2]
- 443 million school days are lost each year due to water-related diseases.[3]
- Half of the world's hospital beds are filled with people suffering from a water-related disease.[4]
- The average container for water collection in Africa, the jerry can, weighs over 18 kilograms (40 pounds) when full.[5]
- Globally we use 70 percent of our water sources for agriculture and irrigation, and only 10 percent on domestic uses.[6]
- Nearly 1 out of every 5 deaths under the age of 5, worldwide, is due to a water-related disease.[7]
- According to the WHO, for every US-dollar invested in water and sanitation, there is an economic return of between USD 3 and USD 34.[8]
- The UN estimates that Sub-Saharan Africa alone loses 40 billion hours per year collecting water; the same as an entire year's labor in all of France.[9]

1   WHO/UNICEF Joint Monitoring Programme for Water Supply and Sanitation; Progress on Sanitation and Drinking Water 2010.
2   WHO/UNICEF Joint Monitoring Programme for Water Supply and Sanitation; 2015 Report and MDG Assessment.
3   UNDP Human Development Report 2006.
4   UNEP / UN-Habitat; Sick water? The central role of wastewater management in sustainable development.
5   Jerry cans carry approx. 5 gallons of water so if a single gallon of water weighs 8.3 pounds, 5 gallons are 41.5 pounds.
6   AQUASTAT. Food and Agriculture Organization of the United Nations; Water Use.
7   WHO/UNICEF; Diarrhoea: Why children are still dying and what can be done, 2009.
8   World Health Organization; Executive Summary of Costs and benefits of water and sanitation improvements at the global level.
9   UNDP; Resource Guide on Gender and Climate Change, 2009.

CHAPTER 1 – PROLOGUE:
# Why Does Africa Need Innovative Water Financing Mechanisms?

*Atakilte Beyene and Cush Ngonzo Luwesi*

## 1.1   Introduction

'Where there is no water there is no life ... We live by the grace of water' So said Michael Parfit, a freelance writer for the *National Geographic*.[1] Water is the elixir of life; the right, centre and left end of all activities undertaken by any living being. It is the best thermostat, the regulator of temperature of every functioning organism and its ecosystem. But it needs to be in liquid form and come in sufficient quantity. While it controls the environmental health of human society, so necessary for its survival, water also sustains its technological, economic and social development.[2]

Yet, 'many people think that water comes from the tap in the same way milk comes from the cow... When the well is dry, we learn the worth of water'.[3] Therefore, to ensure availability and accessibility of water, innovative approaches to water management are required. The sixteenth-century Italian poet and polymath Leonardo da Vinci described water being as: 'sometimes sharp and sometimes strong, sometimes acid and sometimes bitter, sometimes sweet and sometimes thick or thin, sometimes it is seen bringing hurt or pestilence, sometime health-giving, sometimes poisonous.'[4] True to this quote, Africans consume a kind of water that deserves all da Vinci's qualifications.

In fact, some African watersheds are havens of refreshingly pure, gorgeous and light blue water, while others sadly abound in impure, sulphurous, bitter, red, yellow, green, black, oily and greasy water. Besides, water affects the lives and welfare of close to a billion people in Africa. Almost half of the African population falls sick each year through drinking polluted water. Water is the cause of about 20 deaths in every 100 among the under-5s, and is responsible for the deaths of 20 out of every 1,000 people who die each year in Africa, including more than 1.5 million children from Sub-Saharan Africa.[5] These casualties of cholera and other diarrhoeal/enteric waterborne di-

---

1    Memije-Cruz, 2012
2    Savenije, Hoekstra and van der Zaag, 2014
3    Cyber-nook.com, 2011
4    Witcombe, 1999
5    The Water Project, 2016

seases far outstrip the number of victims of HIV/AIDS, tuberculosis and malaria put together.[6] Nonetheless, water remains a critical natural, economic and social asset for about 85% of poor people living in rural areas, whose main source of livelihood is agriculture.

Water is a basic but indispensable input for economic production and growth, and the development of rural agrarian livelihoods within the context of climate change. The latter decides the fate of most communities living in Sub-Saharan Africa.[7] Most northern, eastern, western and southern African communities face serious development challenges involving water availability, owing to inadequate investment in water infrastructure, insufficient development and mismanagement of water resources, the lack of water allocation policies and emergency interventions.[8] As corollaries, water-related natural disasters (mainly disease, flood and drought), food insecurity and poverty hamper economic development and social welfare in most African communities.[9] Hence, Clarke and King[10] could rightly declare that 'ease of access to water, the efficiency with which resources are used, the capacity of people to benefit and the health of the environment that determine what is known as "Water Poverty".'

Ensuring water availability in the near future presents a great challenge for most African governments, owing to the ever-increasing population size and poverty, water demand for food production and other economic activities, which are under threat of environmental change.[11] Without a roadmap for water development and without better administration and management of its resources, African communities are stuck with 'water poverty'. Deliberate decisions to invest, manage, maintain and conserve water and related resources along the urban-rural economy continuum are key to maintaining a level of 'water security' in Africa.[12] Happily, communities and their governments are working towards creating an environment that will be conducive to cooperation and investment to ensure the availability of this scarce resource.[13] This will enable both present and future generations to have equal access to the same resource. However, there is a need to halt the current trend towards water depletion. As well as stepping up measures designed to tackle water use efficiency and conservation, the African population itself needs to be encouraged to change its mindset and behaviour towards using and saving water.[14] There is finally a need for financing and governance systems that would overhaul the quality of water productivity and the overall economic growth with improved social welfare.[15]

---

6    Eurogeosurveys, 2016.
7    UNEP, 2002
8    Goh, 2012
9    Rees,
10   Clarke and King, 2004
11   The Water Project, 2016
12   Bamutaze, Thiemman and Foerch, 2014
13   GWP, 2015
14   Gilg and Barr, 2006
15   Biamah, 2010

## 1.2    Need for New Governance of the Water Sector

Water is both an environmental and a societal resource, a public good and a commercial commodity. Its governance requires an integrated approach towards ensuring sustainable provision of quality water resources for ecological, economic and social services.[16] The application of the principles of conservation ecology, economic rationalization and financial sustainability is therefore essential to enable the optimization of costs and benefits from water investments.[17] But why is such governance indispensable for Africa's survival?

In most climate zones freshwater availability fluctuates with the seasons and is scarce during some months each year. Given the vital nature of water for humans, all societies located in such climate zones developed ways to arrange and secure access to water for domestic and productive uses. Those societies that survived over time found ways to use water in a sustainable manner, or at least allowed the water resource to regenerate itself and did not destroy the natural cycle.[18]

First, as an environmental resource, water is finite, vulnerable and scarce. Figure 1.1 indicates that the majority of water resources are salty, found in the oceans and lakes (97.5%), while part of the freshwater is locked in glaciers and ice lands (2.1%). Only 0.4% out of the 141,870 $km^3$ of the world's water reserves is available for production and consumption by more than 7 billion human beings and innumerable billions of other forms of life.[19]

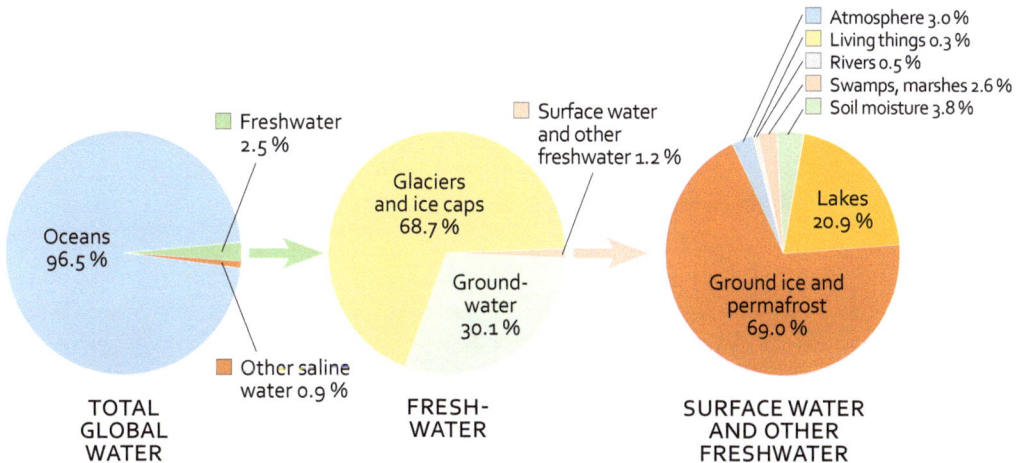

**Figure 1.1.** Rainwater distribution across the globe

Another ecological issue is the inequitable distribution of precipitation and water bodies. That is the major challenge facing Africa and the global society in the course of

16    Falkenmark and Rockström, 2004
17    Harris, 2008
18    Savenije, Hoekstra and van der Zaag, 2014
19    Eurogeosurveys, 2016; and Kundzewicz, Mata, Arnell, Doll, Kabat, Jimenez and Shiklomanov, 2007

climate change, aside from dealing with physical water scarcity.[20] According to some hydrologists, lakes and rivers are havens for 94.6% and 5.4%, respectively, of accessible global freshwater.[21] The Amazon and the Congo basins carry 15% and 3.5% of total river flow on Earth, yet serve only 0.4% and 2.5% of the planet's humans, respectively. North and Latin America, with 4.8% and 8.6% of the global population, are been gifted with 17.5% and 26% of the global accessible freshwater resources, respectively. Yet, Asia and North Africa, which account for almost 60% and 2.5%, respectively, of the world's population have to make do with only 30% and 0.3% of the accessible global freshwater, respectively.[22,23] Besides, most arid and semi-arid lands are highly populated, yet they receive less rainfall than the rest of the planet et al., 2017).[24] Scientists believe that climate change and its drivers, including higher urbanization rates, deforestation and water over-abstraction for agriculture and livestock production, are among those factors explaining the increase in solar radiation and the global warming phenomenon, as well as the dispersion of clouds, and thus the changing patterns in weather and precipitations.[25] These factors seriously impact on the world's water distribution, its supply and demand. Addressing these problems will be critical in achieving the new and ambitious Sustainable Development Goals (SDGs) adopted by the United Nations in 2015. SDG Goal 6 relates to water, and includes targets for improving access to sanitation, reducing water pollution, improving water use efficiency, and making water use more sustainable.[26]

From an economic point of view, among productive sectors there is high competition for water resources ownership and use for agricultural, industrial and livestock production, power generation, other human livelihoods and consumption. This competition often leads to conflicts among regions, countries and communities over water control.[27] In August 1995, Ismail Serageldin, the then World Bank Vice-President, warned the global community: 'If the wars of this century were fought over oil, the wars of the next century will be fought over water – unless we change our approach to managing this precious and vital resource'.[28]

This attracted the attention of the American media and others to raise awareness about the level of attention needed to help address water issues. A new Global Water Partnership (GWP) was thus born as catalyst for policy debates on a comprehensive approach to the management of water issues. The partnership was launched with a secretariat in Stockholm, to provide guidance to world leaders on integrated water resource management (IWRM) (for more information see.[29] But what does the future hold?

20   Bonell, 2008.
21   Learner.org, 2016
22   Shiklomanov, 1993
23   Roudi-Fahimi, Creel and De Souza, 2002
24   Luwesi, Shisanya and Obando, 2017
25   Shisanya and Khayesi, 2007
26   World Bank, 2016.
27   Solomon, 2010
28   Förch, Winnegge and Thiemann, 2005
29   For more information visit Serageldin (2012) webpage

Yes, future projections of the future population growth and business trends call for a drastic change in policy interventions. Clarke and King simulated the world's water withdrawals by the year 2025 using available sector data from 1950 to 1995.[30] In their *first scenario*, with no policy intervention or limitation in the water sector, water withdrawals would grow from 1,400 km³ (1950) and 3,800 km³ (1995) to 5,270 km³ by 2025. Population growth was set to 4.6% a year, irrigation expansion was expected to be 39% and business was assumed to increase at the same pace as earlier (Figure 1.2).

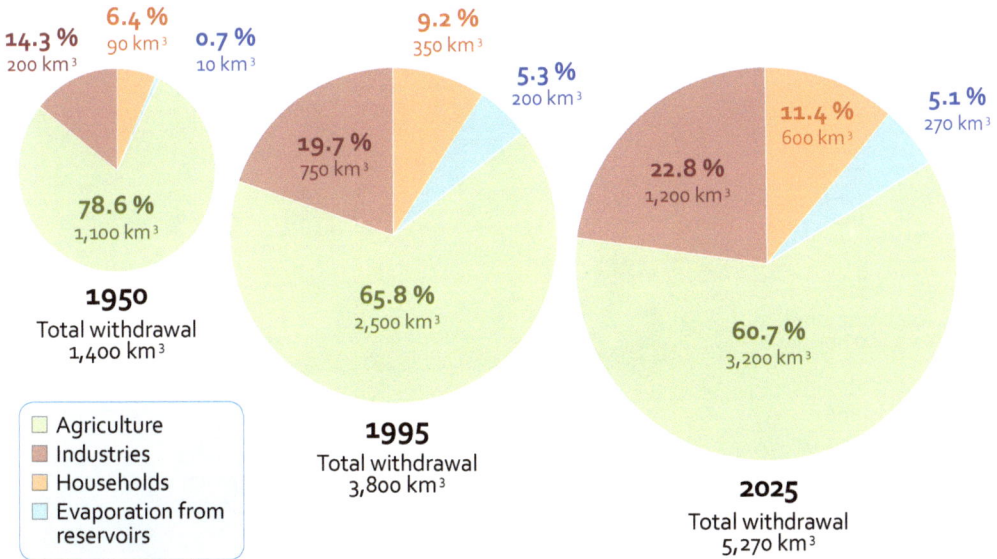

Figure 1.2. Water withdrawals without policy intervention.[31]

The *second scenario* indicated 4,300 km³ water withdrawals by the year 2025. Under this scenario, the growth in population and business would maintain the same pace, but there would be less compliance on dam building standards to reduce water wastage in irrigation, so that the growth of the agricultural sector would be limited (Table 1.1).

|                              | 1950  | 1995  | 2025  |
|------------------------------|-------|-------|-------|
| **Agriculture**              | 1,100 | 2,500 | 2,300 |
| **Industries**               | 200   | 750   | 900   |
| **Households**               | 90    | 350   | 900   |
| **Evaporation from reservoirs** | 10 | 200   | 200   |
| **Total withdrawal**         | 1,400 | 3,800 | 4,300 |

Table 1.1. Water withdrawals with limited policy intervention.[32]

---

30   Clarke and King, 2004
31   Adapted from Clarke and King (2004).
32   Adapted from Clarke and King (2004).

Consequently, political leaders are likely to set policies that would enable efficient water management to sustain its availability and accessibility. This decision would be made after it comes to their notice that the limited size of irrigated land leads to chronic food shortage, malnutrition, limited water and sanitation services, along with water-borne diseases and ecological disasters.

*In the last scenario* water withdrawals were anticipated to be 4,170 km³ by 2025, and involved the implementation of integrated management of water resources (Figure 1.3).

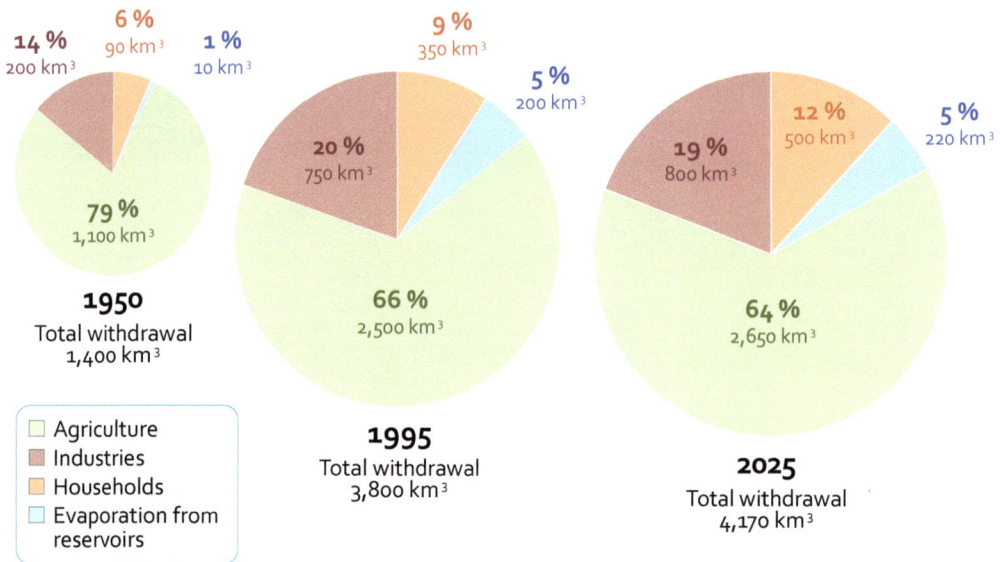

**Figure 1.3.** Water withdrawal, with integrated water resource management[33]

Under this last scenario, effective equipment is widely available for drilling, treating and distributing water. Water-borne diseases are supposedly eradicated thanks to the provision and use of effective water and sanitation services. Though water consumption would be a universal right, the enhanced value of water may lead to a price tag that could be a burden for the poor. Therefore, the use of pro-poor 'green' water-saving mechanisms and other financial innovations would be highly recommended to enable social equity and to alleviate poverty.[34] Therefore, 'we need a frank conversation about water development, in order to raise funds for capital expenditure in water infrastructure for the development of 'blue' water resources' (see below).[35] There is also a big search on for innovative financing mechanisms for alternative blue water options, sometimes referred to as 'green water credits' (GWC), 'green water saving' (GWS) or 'green water management' (GWM) schemes. [36]

---

33   Adapted after Clarke and King, 2004
34   Akombo, Luwesi, Shisanya and Obando, 2014
35   Kauffman, Droogers, Odada, Macharia, Gicheru and Dijkshoorn, 2007
36   Luwesi, Shisanya and Obando, 2007; Malesu, Oduor and Odhiambo, 2007; and Droogers, 2006

## 1.3    A Call for Green Water Development and Management

Owing to the depletion of land resources in most water catchment areas, water resources need to be developed and managed rationally, everywhere and at all times, using both infrastructure and other financial resources to make water available to all. 'The great challenge we face is to get to business not as usual.[37]

There is an urgent need for innovative economic and financial instruments to develop technologies that go beyond the government targets, as well as for plans and budgets that enhance water development performance in poor rural contexts.[38] These new tools require novel thinking and risk-taking approaches from water sector actors, who need to come up with new paradigms that promote innovative partnerships aimed at sustainable funding-opportunity sourcing and water resource development, as well as the efficient management of those resources in both market and non-market settings.[39]

Water development by means of GWS schemes has proved to be climate-resilient and capable of providing both socio-economic and environmental incentives for local stakeholders to develop and manage their water resources using participatory approaches.[40] These schemes have proved to be innovative adaptation mechanisms that encourage local stakeholders to cooperate in 'integrated water resources management' (IWRM), mainly in arid and semi-arid lands (ASALs). Here 'green water', the accessible soil moisture generated by plants from rainfall transfer into the soil for their own use, is the largest freshwater resource, but it can only be used in situ, by plants.[41] Globally, this green water represents two-thirds of soil moisture generated by plants and is a major contributor to surface runoff, interflow and groundwater, which are referred to as 'blue water'. Blue water constitutes one-tenth of accessible soil moisture from direct transfer of rainfall into the soil (Figure 1.4). Through GWS schemes, downstream and upstream stakeholders learn to cooperate and effectively develop, manage, allocate and conserve their water resources.[42] This increases their groundwater reserves, and as a corollary generates extensive interflow and surface runoff, which definitely enhances the sustainability and resilience of the people's livelihoods in the course of climate change.[43]

---

37    Berntell, 2007
38    Mathenge, Luwesi, Shisanya, Mahiri, Akombo and Mutiso, 2014
39    Luwesi, Kinuthia, Mutiso, Akombo, Doke and Ruhakana, 2015
40    Reij, Tappan and Smale, 2009
41    Luwesi and Badr, 2013; and Falkenmark and Rockström, 2004
42    Bastiaanssen and Bingfang, 2008
43    Kauffman, Droogers, Odada, Macharia, Gicheru, Dijkshoorn, 2007

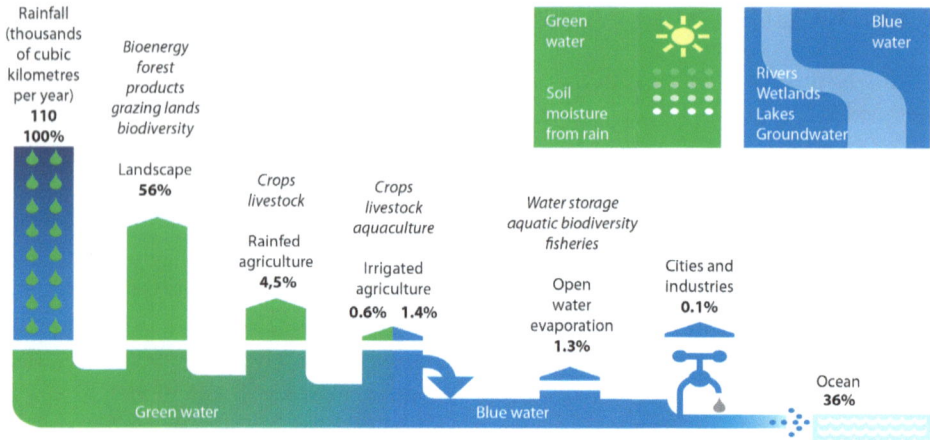

**Figure 1.4.** Blue and green water distribution across the globe. "Green water" refers to rainwater stored in the soil or on vegetation, which cannot be diverted to a different use. "Blue water" is surface and groundwater, which can be stored and diverted for a specific purpose. [44]

Whether implemented as water and land conservation measures, cropping and tree planting techniques, and payments for watershed services (PWS), GWS schemes remain effective mechanisms for preparedness, adaptation and mitigation of climate impacts using available resources. [45] Through these schemes, local stakeholders learn to safeguard their water resources using simultaneous and real water-saving programmes that sustain the management of irrigation schemes, inform decision-making on resource allocation and assist in disaster mitigation in water-scarce areas.[46] They are also pro-poor schemes, initiated by local stakeholders at the lowest level of environmental management, in lieu of poverty alleviation mechanisms initiated by government institutions and/or their international development partners.[47] GWS schemes are thus more than simple land-use practices, soil-conservation measures or micro-financial schemes. They are part of a long-term water resources development strategy that addresses both water scarcity and rural poverty through planning and management of all available water resources by local stakeholders.[48] GWS schemes are therefore part of an innovative 'climate-resilient development' programme that seeks to combat poverty while conserving the environment using fair payments for watershed services by local stakeholders.[49]

> *This past decade has seen a rise of a more participative instrument, Payments for Watershed Services (PWS). Here, those who manage the land (i.e. service providers) and those who benefit from cleaner and better watershed services (i.e. service users)*

---

44    UNEP, 2011 (Source: after Molden 2007)
45    Porras, Grieg-Gran and Meijerink, 2007
46    Grieg-Gran, Noel and Porras, 2006
47    Luwesi, Kinuthia, Mutiso, Akombo, Doke and Ruhakana, 2015
48    Chukalla, Krol and Hoekstra, 2015
49    Porras, Grieg-Gran and Meijerink, 2007

*are brought together. "Providers" receive payments from downstream "users" (which includes local governments, the private sector and other interest groups) to invest in better management, and often representatives of both groups meet to discuss problems and solutions leading to better water governance.* [50]

To be effective, GWS payments need to be translated into farmer's culture, which requires a drastic behaviour change in the provision of ecosystem services at the watershed level. The performance of GWS schemes combined with investments in rainwater harvesting would result in an increase of 50% or more in the one-tenth accessible blue water in streams, lakes and groundwater. That is when a green revolution in Africa would be possible to increase food and grain reserves, possibly as happened in the 1970s in south-east Asia.[51]

## 1.4    Adequate Financing System for Rural Water Development

The development of green water resources requires sustainable provision of green water services by local service providers and the full cost of these services to be recovered from water users' income. It involves not only adequate and reliable cash flow from a quality service, but also efficient and effective financial management.[52] A quality service is essential to ensure the willingness of water users to pay. Customers' willingness to pay for bottled water (versus tap water) and mobile phone services (versus landline phone services) in many African countries has proved that users really yearn to see quality service prior to making a decision to pay.[53] Another factor leading to such a decision is efficiency. This is indispensable when seeking to limit public fund evasion (through corruption or subsidies), and laziness that leads to the failure of the whole economy. This is well illustrated by comparing efficient private corporations and inefficient public services in Africa, especially in terms of time management.[54] Finally, effectiveness is required in order to mobilize more resources using alternative funding sources to close the gap in financing, capacity and engagement. Adequate financing strategies are needed for planning costs, revenues and repayable finances, in order to increase financial discipline and creditworthiness, and to close the gap between costs and incomes, funding and expenditure.[55] A strong governance system and viable administrative structures, with continuous communication and marketing, will help address sustainability issues by closing the gap in capacity and engagement with the personnel and local stakeholders. Finally, the gap in project financing will be closed only if financial needs and constraints in the water sector are properly identified and addressed.[56]

50    Porras, Aylward and Denge, 2013
51    GRAIN Briefing, 2007
52    AGRA, 2009
53    Preston, 1997
54    Oduol, Hotta, Shinkai and Tsuji, 2006
55    Mcgill, 2006
56    Furubo, 2009

With regards to closing the financing gap, it cannot be overemphasized that financial discussions in the water sector often focus on full cost recovery in urban areas through tariffs, and on lobbying donors and international financial institutions (IFIs) to spend more money on water.[57] Even water development in rural Africa usually relies on the '3Ts': *tariffs* (by service users), *taxation* (by taxpayers) and *transfer* (from development partners). The cost of operations and maintenance (O&M) are not yet fully covered by the current spending on water management and service provision through user fees (tariffs), domestic taxpayers (taxation) and/or donor support (transfer) in many African countries.[58] Besides, water sector management in Africa is widely dominated by political approaches towards its governance and management. This political capture of the water sector impedes engineering and economic innovations needed for water services development. It also discourages community involvement in water resources management.[59] To allow for technical and economic solutions to water scarcity, water sector governance and management need constant scrutiny and financial contributions from local stakeholders for their sustainability.[60] Weak public participation in financing the sustainable development of water resources and services justifies the inadequacy of the financial resources allocated to the water sector for physical investment, operations and maintenance. Therefore, the implementation of soft components of water governance is required, alongside relevant engineering, economic and financial instruments. This would alleviate the burden of poor prioritization and inadequate strategic financial assets – desperately needed in case of drought and other environmental disasters.[61]

These strategic finances and innovations are crucial in a changing environment that is dominated by the climate-change impacts discourse, and in which investments in the water sector are perceived as bound up with politics and high financial risks.[62] The water resource management (WRM) sub-sector is largely conceived of as a public function, and it is thus difficult to ensure funding from private investors. However, the water and sanitation services (WSS) sub-sector is essentially capital intensive and requires long-term funding with slow-paced cash flows, thus making it highly risky for private investment. Besides, revenue collected in the water sector rarely covers O&M costs, and is therefore unattractive to private investors.[63] Water sector actors are therefore encouraged to create innovative approaches to financing their current and capital expenditure in the course of climate change.

Nonetheless, Mcgray et al. (2007) suggest an adaptation response for designing water development programmes.[64] This should take into account two main drivers

---

57   WSP, 2012
58   WASREB, 2014
59   Meijerink, Muchena, Njue, Noel, Onduru and Porras, 2007
60   WASREB, 2011
61   Luwesi, 2010
62   Luwesi, Shisanya and Obando, 2017
63   IBNET, 2012
64   Mcgray, Hammill, Bradley, Schipper and Parry, 2007

that increase the effectiveness of water projects: (i) the existing capacity of the affected community, and (ii) the level of information about projected climate impacts. It is recommended that the programme should involve both upstream and downstream stakeholders in the planning process.[65] Public-private partnership (PPP) is another prerequisite for implementation of water development programmes. Government institutions should work together with private agencies for the benefit of both upstream and downstream stakeholders.[66] Prior to setting up physical interventions, water sector regulators should first seek the enhancement of the capacity of local stakeholders and corporates (i.e. water suppliers, associations of water users and irrigators, farmers' cooperatives and banks) for the sustainable management of their water resources in the course of climate change. The greater the stakeholders' capacity, the lower their vulnerability; the lower local stakeholders' vulnerability, the higher the investments in addressing underlying causes of vulnerability, and the lower the climate impacts on the affected community will be.[67] This book is designed to provide some useful tools and approaches that will enable African water managers to achieve higher investment in water infrastructure and bolster the resilience of communities that are affected by climate change.

## 1.5    Rationale for Innovative Water Finance in Africa

The current situation of water supply and water resources management in Africa is quite worrying, owing to the inadequate development of infrastructure and the financial resources that could ensure the supply of water and sanitation services to everyone, everywhere and at all times. In general, about 40% of the rural population and 60% of the urban population have access to clean potable water; around 20% of these are urban poor. Less than half of these households are connected to sanitation systems. The inadequate access to clean water increases the risk of water-borne diseases and contamination from untreated wastewater and inadequate disposal of sewage.[68]

Water availability is threatened by poor water resource management, given the recurring cycles of drought and flood, the increasing water pollution, high population growth and uncontrolled water withdrawals, to name but a few factors.[69] The resulting low water flows and the siltation of dam reservoirs is a major cause of energy disruption, leading to electricity rationing in many major cities.[70] In such circumstances, the water companies are forced to look for alternative energy sources and funding to secure water provision during periods of drought. This has raised concern about innovative financing instruments, which can be accessed at affordable market interest rates.

---

65    Geertsma, Wilschut and Kauffman, 2010
66    Obando, Luwesi, Mathenge, Kinuthia, Wambua, Mutiso and Bader, 2015
67    Mcgray, Hammill, Bradley, Schipper and Parry, 2007
68    Briceño-G., Smits and Foster, 2008
69    Kundzewicz, Mata, Arnell, Doll, Kabat, Jimenez... Shiklomanov, 2007
70    Luwesi and Cofie, 2015

Moreover, the increasing number of taxes and other fees due to government institutions is of concern to water service providers as they strive to achieve efficiency and equity in the water sector.[71] The latter provide a universal right of access to water for every citizen, and thus compel every government to drastically reduce the number of people without sustainable access to safe drinking water and sanitation services in accordance with its own legislation.[72] That is why most African governments are reforming their water sector governance and, at the same time, developing plans – with a target of 100% – for securing the delivery of water and sanitation services by the year 2050. Through these reforms, water resource management is likely to improve, thus resulting in a fair distribution of resources.[73] Kenya, for instance, established a multi-year framework known as the National Water Sector Strategy (NWSS) to implement these targets. For the effective implementation of the NWSS, a transfer of finance and know-how has been sought by the ministry of water and irrigation from other sectors.[74] There has also been a dialogue between politics, administration, science and industry to achieve significant improvement in the energy and water supply and in the sanitation services.[75]

In such a context, Kenya's two main water sector associations – the Water Service Providers' Association (WASPA) and the Kenya Water Industry Association (KWIA) – asked the Kenya Water Institute (KEWI) to train their membership (mainly water service providers) in how to set up a professional and political dialogue in order to raise funds and improve water and sanitation service delivery. In 2010, they finally agreed on the terms of reference. These envisaged strengthening the partnership between the associations and their members to offer customized services for water, sanitation and energy. This would allow the associations (WASPA and KWIA) to extend their influence among their members and improve their competencies in building partnerships and sharing information, developing organizational structures, advocating for their members' interests, and establishing the basis for professionalization in the water sector.[76]

In pursuit of this partnership, Bfz gGmbH (a German school of business) was sub-contracted by KEWI to initiate a project to strengthen the partnership between the members of the two main associations of the Kenyan water sector (the SWAP project). Two workshops were convened and co-organized by Bfz/SWAP project, in collaboration with WaterCap (an East African network), in Mombasa on 7-11 November 2011. These workshops were first mandated to strengthen the partnership between the water service providers (WSPs) and their association, WASPA; and then between WASPA and the Water Resources Management Authority (WRMA) and the water resource users' associations (WRUAs), for cooperation in the management of water resources. The training workshops primarily targeted financial managers and managing directors who are members of WASPA, and managers from the WRMA regional offices.

---

71  IUCN, 2016
72  Republic of Kenya, 2002
73  Republic of Kenya, 2007
74  Ngigi and Macharia, 2007
75  Republic of Kenya, 2010
76  Luwesi, 2011

During these two workshops, the financial managers and managing directors of Kenyan water utilities highlighted four major expectations, addressing the theme 'innovative ways of financing the water sector'. These included: (i) financial opportunities arising from water infrastructure development and resources management; (ii) innovative fund-raising and economic innovations for water services development and provision; (iii) strategic leadership communication and marketing for successful engagement and financial resources mobilization; and (iv) capacity building, knowledge sharing and networking in economics and finance. Box 1.2 highlights the expectations of the participants of the workshops under each of the above themes. These are the true motivation for this book, whose scope goes beyond Kenya to encompass the entire African continent. Therefore, this book is expected to be a comprehensive and timely collection, designed to provide essential approaches and tools to be used by policy makers, managing directors and financial managers – in the developing world generally, and Africa in particular. It will help them understand the new context of the water sector reforms and their repercussions in sourcing market and non-market funding and investment opportunities for efficient management and development of their water resources.

| Funding Opportunities | Economic Innovations and Fund-Sourcing |
|---|---|
| • Different financing options to sustain operations<br>• Innovative ways of funding water projects<br>• Sourcing funds from the private sector for water resources management<br>• Governmental budget allocations to water services and water resources management | • The most important variables for water pricing and tariff setting<br>• Techniques for sustainable cost recovery using water charges and fees<br>• Alternative options for improving non-revenue water and wastage avoidance<br>• Other options for enhancing performance |
| Strategic Finances Mobilization | Capacity Building and Knowledge Sharing |
| • Strategic methods for financial planning<br>• Strategic leadership for ensuring the viability of water utilities<br>• Water governance and engagement for financing the water sector<br>• Communication skills and knowledge for a WSP financial management | • Best practices in managing the water sector<br>• Challenges facing others in funding the water sector and raising revenues<br>• Alternative options for sustainable water management and financing<br>• Knowledge and experience sharing |

**Box 1.2.** Major Expectations of Water Sector Managers

Regarding financial opportunities arising from water infrastructure and resources management, water managers wanted to understand innovative ways of funding water projects, with a special focus on different financing options available for the water sector. They also required different options for financing water infrastructure development and other water sector financing opportunities available for water resources management. They stressed the need for water development in the context of public-private partnerships so as to lift that burden on the public sector by sourcing private funds for water resources management, including water trust funds and investment in water utilities. Some African watersheds are havens of refreshing, clean, gorgeous and light blue water, while others sadly abound in impure, sulphurous, bitter, red, yellow, green, black, oily and greasy water.

Deliberate decisions to invest, manage, maintain and conserve water and related resources along the urban-rural economy continuum are key to maintaining a level of 'water security' in Africa. Consequently, political leaders are likely to set policies that would enable efficient water management to sustain its availability and accessibility. Moreover, understanding opportunities that can be used to finance water resources management other than the routine revenue streams (the 3Ts) currently used in most African countries would enable new water sources to be 'tapped' without unnecessarily burdening poor farmers and other key stakeholders. However, the proponents of financial innovations should determine the extent to which infrastructure development and water resources management can be financed. The focus on new ways of accessing finance for the development and management of water resources was justified by the fact that this sub-sector generates public goods instead of economic profits.

Besides, water managers need advice on how to sustain recurring managerial operations for water services development and provision. Since water is coming to be in great demand as a right, its funding levels should also be raised to measure up to the needs. Therefore, a clear understanding of the various avenues for sourcing cheap funds should be sought to finance water provision. These sustainable financing mechanisms can only be achieved through an accurate prediction of the resources' availability and the expansion of projects to improve water services within the areas of coverage. Water managers thus need guidance on how to acquire project financing without having to offer the traditional collateral required by the banking sector. These are some of the new approaches and innovative ways being used in the building, energy and transport sectors to finance the development of their networks for the sustainable provision of services beyond available sources of asset financing and government budget financing. This would help them address the challenges faced in sourcing funds and mobilizing resources to improve water availability and sanitation services. In this regard, economic water innovations were needed for both water pricing and resource optimization. Understanding the most important variables of water pricing and how to set cost recovery tariffs would ensure the sustainability of the water companies and institutions. This includes the practical application of water valuation methods; and the control of production costs through optimization of energy efficiency and other resources utilization.

Several expectations were voiced by water managers on strategic leadership and communication for participatory water governance and financial resources mobilization. These included: (i) understanding the key to water governance and the financing of viable utilities and water sector structures; (ii) providing insight into the business of various water sector institutions and services in a decentralized legal and institutional framework; (iii) expanding knowledge on the financial management of water infrastructure and operations; (iv) providing strategic methods for planning and managing the mobilization of financial resources; (v) acquiring marketing and communication skills and knowledge to enhance networking and financial resources; (vi) understanding the role of managers in ensuring the viability of water companies and institutions; (vii) discovering how effective marketing management and communication work in the water sector; (viii) proposing sustainable ways of improving water and sewerage services vis-à-vis current tariffs and business growth needs; (ix) identifying innovative ways of motivating the workforce to enhance its performance, despite low salaries due to inadequate revenue and education; and (x) learning how to create platforms for engaging new partners.

Finally, when it came to capacity building, water managers recommended alternative options for learning, knowledge sharing and networking to ensure sustainable water financing and management. This required creating a conducive environment for learning, knowledge sharing and networking in the water sector, with a focus on key research areas of water finance in the sector. Therefore, water managers needed to understand how to address research problems in the water finance area, and/or to anticipate them, without any input from universities. For instance, it was said that water managers can solve water sector challenges by following financial trends in the sector so as to design a strategy for funding and managing water companies and institutions sustainably. Getting such information gathered and shared would enable them to learn new lessons on challenges faced in terms of fund raising and revenue collection for improved water finance. But these managers would needed to collaborate and interact with all the stakeholders in the water sector, including in academia, to enhance their water resources management and services provision. The following section summarizes the key concepts to be learned by water managers and that constitute the basis for this book.

## 1.6   Outline of the Book

This book is published in three volumes. Volume 1 sets the context of the calls for financial innovation in the water sector. It introduces the issues of governance that have led to reform of the water sector in many African countries, as well as the potential financing challenges facing water resources managers and water service providers (Chapters 1–6). The second volume explains how basic economic laws underpinning the profitability, efficiency and sustainability of the management of water companies and institutions are applied to match the best financial sources with the most pressing needs (Chapters 7–11). And the third volume unveils how some companies and institutions have explored financing opportunities arising from the new environment to raise funds to meet both their operating and their capital needs with minimum financial risk (Chapters 12–17).

After this prologue entitled 'Why does Africa need innovative water financing mechanisms?,' Chapter 2 provides an overview of the water sector development and financing in Africa by tackling some challenges facing the sector and opportunities available for a green revolution to take place in Africa. Chapter 3 unveils the basic principles of integrated water resources management (IWRM) that should guide water development and financing: efficiency, equity and sustainability. Then follows an analysis of the legal and market requirements for financing the water sector by focusing on institutional aspects, security issues and financial options accruing from the water sector reforms in Kenya (Chapter 4). Chapter 5 gives some guidelines for resource mobilization in the water sector through adoption of societal marketing, communication and engagement with local stakeholders. An example is drawn from the CGIAR research programme on 'Water, Land and Ecosystems' (WLE). This volume closes with Chapter 6, entitled 'Women in Water Finance Concept', which provides a gendered perspective of water finance in Africa.

Volume II continues with the state of the art on innovative water financing mechanisms. Chapter 7 introduces the concept of financial instruments and operations in the water sector. It reminds the reader how tiny (and sometimes unpredictable) is funding from government ministries, the public trust funds and international development partners. Hence, innovative ways of financing operations and assets can supplement water management and businesses by increasing internal savings through a snowball effect of public–private partnerships, commercial loans and concessions, and other financial facilities. The public–private partnerships encompass such innovative schemes as Build, Operate and Lease (BOL), Build, Operate and Sell (BOS) and Build, Operate and Transfer (BOT), to name but a few. The following chapters cover several aspects of the economics of water financing and management. They elicit key principles behind the economic profitability and efficiency of water projects (Chapter 8), discuss a probabilistic cost-benefit analysis for the economic viability of blue water projects (Chapter 9), and unveil an unconventional cost-benefit analysis based on contingent valuation methods to evaluate the feasibility of green water investments and especially payments for watershed services (Chapter 10). Finally, Chapter 11 discloses some determinants of access to irrigated agricultural credits to build models that work for the rural poor in Northern Ghana.

Volume III starts with an epilogue that presents opportunities and challenges for water resources management, as well as related financing issues that need to be addressed in the near future in Africa (Chapter 12). Chapter 13 expands on that concept by tackling financial strategies and innovations introduced in the management of water. Chapters 14 and 15 present case studies on the funding and transfer mechanisms of irrigation schemes in West and East Africa. These chapters show the drivers behind irrigation financing, as well as the opportunities and the linkages by drawing on examples from eastern and western Africa. Nonetheless this chapter remains relevant for other regions of Africa. After reading the book, readers will realize that innovative water finance is not a 'fairy-tale ending' but a day-to-day reality that needs to be customized for each context. Chapter 16 elaborates on a series of success stories of innovative leadership, marketing and enhanced creditworthiness from the Kenyan water sector, especially from the water and sanitation companies from Embu, Nyeri and Murang'a counties. This chapter reminds that water managers need effective methods of marketing and communication as well as engagement skills to build partnerships with actors from the banking sector, microfinance, NGOs and private companies, to invite government agencies and bilateral/multilateral development partners to unveil their strategies and the opportunities they could offer the water sector. Finally, Chapter 17 unfolds "sustainable provision and financing of groundwater irrigation in African drylands'. It recommends an innovative technology that integrates Indian groundwater storage technology (Holiya) with Danish pumping technology (by Grundfos Lifelink) and Kenyan mobile money transfer technology (known as M-Pesa) for agricultural water development and financing in arid and semi-arid lands.

# References

AGRA. [Alliance for a Green Revolution in Africa]. 2009. AGRA: Early Accomplishments, Foundation for Growth. Available at: http://www.agra-alliance.org (Accessed on 13.07.2010).

Akombo, R.A., Luwesi, C.N., Shisanya, C.A. and Obando, J.A. 2014. Green Water Credits for Sustainable Agriculture and Forestry in Arid and Semi-Arid Tropics of Kenya. Journal of Agri-Food and Applied Sciences (JAAS), Vol. 2 (4): 86-92.

Bamutaze, Y., Thiemman, S. and Foerch, G. 2014. Integrated Watershed Management for Urban Water Security: Integrated Watershed Management – a Tool for Urban Water Security Workshop Results from Mbale, Uganda. Berlin: Freie Universitat Berlin and IWM Expert GmbH

Bastiaanssen, W. and Bingfang, W. 2008. Hai Tide: Tapping Green Water in Northern China. Stockholm Water Front No 1, April 2008:12-13.

Berntell, A. 2007. Getting to Business Not as Usual. Stockholm Water Front No 1, April 2008:1-2

Biamah, E.K. 2010. Current and future responses to drivers of change for water availability and use for agriculture. CTA Annual Seminar 2010- Closing the Knowledge Gap: Integrated Water Management for Sustainable Agriculture. Wageningen: The ACP-EU Technical Centre for Agricultural and Rural Cooperation (CTA), pp. 5-6. Available at: http://annualseminar2010.cta.int (Accessed on 13.02.2013)

Bonell, M. 2008. The role of the HELP programme. In: P. Meire, M. Coenen, C. Lombardo, M. Robba and R. Sacile (Eds.), Integrated Water Management. Earth and Environmental Sciences (Series IV) – Vol. 80. Dordrecht: Springer (formerly Kluwer Academic Publishers) in conjunction with the NATO Public Diplomacy Division, pp. 247-262.

Briceño-G., C., Smits, K. and Foster, V. 2008. Africa Infrastructure Country Diagnostic (AICD), Summary of Background Paper 15: Financing Public Infrastructure in Sub-Saharan Africa: Patterns, Issues, and Options. Washington, DC: The World Bank.

Chukalla, A.D. Krol, M.S. and Hoekstra, A.Y. 2015. Green and blue water footprint reduction in irrigated agriculture: effect of irrigation techniques, irrigation strategies and mulching. Hydrol. Earth Syst. Sci., 19, 4877–4891. Available at: www.hydrol-earth-syst-sci.net/19/4877/2015/ (Accessed on 10. 10.2016)

Clarke, R. and King, J. 2004. The Atlas of Water. London: Earthscan Publications Ltd.

Cyber-nook.com. 2011. A quote of Poor Richard's Almanac, 1746 (Accessed on 11.09.2011)

Droogers, P. 2006. Basin scale hydrology scenarios to explore Green Water Credits opportunities. In: Dent, D. (Ed.), First Green Water Credits Workshop. Wageningen: ISRIC - World Soil Information.

Eurogeosurveys. 2016. Wonder water: The value of water. Available at: http://www.eurogeosurveys.org/wp-content/uploads/2016/03/Water-Book-Layout_full-low-double-no-print.pdf (Accessed on 06.03.2017)

Falkenmark, M. and Rockström, J. 2004. Balancing water for humans and nature. London: Earthscan.

Förch, G., Winnegge, R. and Thiemann, S. (eds.). 2005. DAAD Alumni Summer School 2005: Topics of Integrated Water Resources Management. Weiterbilding in Siegen, No. 18.

Furubo, J-E. 2009. Evaluation and Performance Audit: Rationale, questions and Methods. Speech at Conference arranged by Cours des Comptes (France). Available at: www.riksrevionen.se (Accessed on 13.07.2010).

Geertsma, R., Wilschut, L. and Kauffman, S. 2010. Review for the Green Water Credits Pilot Operation in Kenya. In: Kauffman, S. (ed.), Green Water Credits Report 8. Wageningen: ISRIC - World Soil Information.

Gilg, A. and Barr, S. 2006. Analysis: Behavioural attitudes towards water saving? Evidence from a study of environmental actions. Ecological Economics 57: 400–414. Available at: http://www.sciencedirect.com (Accessed on 13.02.2013)

Goh, A.H.X. 2012. A literature review of the gender-differentiated impacts of climate change on women's and men's assets and well-being in developing countries. CAPRi Working Paper No. 106 (September 2012). Washington, D.C.: International Food Policy Research Institute (IFPRI). Available at: http://dx.doi.org/10.2499/CAPRiWP106 (Accessed on 13.02.2013).

GRAIN Briefing. 2007. A New Green Revolution for Africa?. November 2007 Issue. Available at: http://www.grain.org/briefings/ (Accessed on 13.07.2010).

Grieg-Gran, M., Noel, S. and Porras, I. 2006. Lessons from Payments for Environmental Services. In: D. Dent (ed.), Green Water Credits Report 2. Wageningen: ISRIC - World Soil Information.

GWP. [Global Water Partnership]. 2015. Integrated Water Resources Management in Eastern Africa: Coping with 'Complex Hydrology'. Technical Focus Papers (TFP) No 7. Stockholm: Elanders.

Harris, J.M. 2008. Ecological Macroeconomics: Consumption, Investment and Climate Change. GDAE Working Paper No. 08-02. Available online at URL: http://www.ase.tufts.edu/gdae/ pubs/ wp/08-02EcologMacroEconJuly08.pdf (Accessed on 13.07.2012).

IBNET. [International Benchmarking Network]. 2012. International Benchmarking for Water and Sanitation Utilities. Available at: www.ibnet.org (Accessed on 17.03.2013)

IUCN. [International Union for Conservation of Nature]. 2016. Knowledge for SDG Action in West Asia and North Africa: R-KNOW Water Governance Best Practices within the Water, Energy,Food and Climate Change Nexus. Amman: IUCN- Regional Office for West Asia. Available at: www.iucn.org/westasia (Accessed on 05.03.2017)

Kauffman, S., Droogers, P., Odada, E., Macharia, P., Gicheru, P., Dijkshoorn, J.A. 2007. Green and Blue Water Resources and assessment of Soil and Water Management Scenarios Using an Integrated Modelling Framework. In: Dent, D. (ed.), Green Water Credits Report 3. Wageningen: ISRIC - World Soil Information.

Kundzewicz, Z.W., Mata, L.J., Arnell, N.W., Doll, P., Kabat, P., Jimenez, B., … Shiklomanov, I. A. 2007. Freshwater resources and their management. In M. L. Parry et al. (Eds.), Climate Change 2007: Impacts, Adaptation and Vulnerability. Cambridge: Cambridge University Press.

Learner.org. 2016. The habitable planet: Water Resources. Available at: https://www.learner.org/courses/envsci/unit/pdfs/unit8.pdf (Accessed on 10.11.2016)

Luwesi, C.N. (Ed.). 2011. Innovative Ways in Financing the Water Sector. Final SWAP/bfz Workshop Report. Mombasa: Bfz and WaterCap, 7-11 November 2011. Available at: http://watercap.org/ (Accessed on 17.03.2013)

Luwesi, C.N. 2010. Hydro-economic Inventory in a Changing Environment – An assessment of the efficiency of farming water demand under fluctuating rainfall regimes in semi-arid lands of South-East Kenya. Saarbrüken: Lambert Academic Publishing.

Luwesi, C.N. and Badr, E. 2013. Essentials of implementation of improved green water management in Muooni catchment, Machakos district of Kenya. Journal of Agri-Food and Applied Sciences (JAAS), vol. 1 (2): 63-70.

Luwesi, C.N. and Cofie, O. 2015. Transboundary challenges and opportunities in the Volta basin. Paper presented during CGIAR-WLE Greater Mekong Forum on Water, Food and Energy. 21-23 Oct. 2015. Phnom Penh: Cambodiana Hotel.

Luwesi, C.N., Kinuthia, W., Mutiso, M.N., Akombo, R.A., Doke, D.A. and Ruhakana, A. 2015. Climate change, pro-poor schemes and water inequality - strengths and weaknesses of Kauti irrigation water users' association, Kenya. In: A. Beyene (Ed.), Agricultural Water Institutions in East Africa. Nordiska Afrikainstitutet Current African Issues 63: 43 – 60.

Luwesi, C.N., Shisanya, C.A. and Obando, J.A. 2012. Warming and Greening - The Dilemma Facing Green Water Economy under Changing Micro-Climatic Conditions in Muooni Catchment (Machakos, Kenya). Saarbrüken: Lambert Academic Publishing.

Luwesi, C.N., Shisanya, C.A. and Obando, J.A. 2017. The impact of a warming micro-climate on muooni farmers of Kenya. Agriculture Agriculture vol. 7 (20): 1-21.

Malesu, M.M., Oduor, A.R. and Odhiambo, O.J. (Eds). 2007. Green Water Management Handbook - Rainwater Harvesting For Agricultural Production And Ecological Sustainability. Nairobi: ICRAF [The World Agroforestry Centre].

Mathenge,M.M., Luwesi, C.N., Shisanya, C.A., Mahiri, I., Akombo, R.A., and Mutiso, M.N. 2014. Community participation in water sector governance in Kenya: A performance based appraisal of community water management systems in Ngaciuma-Kinyaritha catchment, Tana basin, Mount Kenya region. International Journal of Innovative Research and Development (IJIRD), vol. 3 (5): 783-792. .

Mcgill, R. 2006. Achieving results: Performance Budgeting in the Least Developed Countries. New York: UNCDF [United Nations Capital Development Fund].

Mcgray, H., Hammill, A., Bradley, R., Schipper, E.L. and Parry, Jo-E. 2007. Weathering the storm: Options for framing adaptation and development. Washington: WRI [World Resource Institute].

Meijerink, G, Muchena, F., Njue, E., Noel, S., Onduru, D. and Porras I. 2007. Political, Institutional and Financial Framework for Green Water Credits in Kenya. In: Dent, D. (ed.), Green Water Credits Report 6. Wageningen: ISRIC - World Soil Information.

Memije-Cruz, L. 2012. Water Shortage. In What Matters Most, 31 March 2012 Issue. Available at: http://www.rainharvest.co.za/wp-content/uploads/2010/11/emerging_water_shortage.jpg (Accessed on 13.02.2013).

Molden, D. (ed.) 2007. Water for life, water for good: A comprehensive assessment of water management in agriculture. International Water Management Institute, Columbo and Earthscan, London.

Ngigi, A. and Macharia, D. 2007. Kenya Water Sector Overview. Nairobi: IT Power East Africa.

Obando, J.A., Luwesi, C.N., Mathenge, J.M., Kinuthia, W., Wambua, P.P., Mutiso, M.N., and Bader, E.O. 2015. Performance assessment and evaluation of community participation in water sector governance - The case of Ngaciuma-Kinyaritha catchment, Mount Kenya region. In: A. Beyene (Ed.), Agricultural Water Institutions in East Africa. Nordiska Afrikainstitutet, Uppsala, Current African Issues 63: 23–42.

Oduol, J.B.A., Hotta, K., Shinkai, S. and Tsuji, M. 2006. Farm size and productive efficiency: Lessons from smallholder farms in Embu District, Kenya. Kyushu University Journal of the Faculty of Agriculture 51 (2): 449-458.

Porras, I. Aylward, B. and Denge, J. 2013. Monitoring payments for watershed services schemes in developing countries. London: International Institute for Environment and Development (IIED), Sustainable Markets Group.

Porras, I., Grieg-Gran, M. and Meijerink, G. 2007. Farmers' Adoption of Soil and Water Conservation: Potential Role of Payments for Watershed Services. In: Dent, D. (ed), Green Water Credits Report 5. Wageningen: ISRIC - World Soil Information.

Preston, M. 1997. Investing in mountains: Innovative mechanisms and promising examples for financing conservation and sustainable development. West Virginia: The Mountain Institute. Available online at URL: http://lib.icimod.org/record/10090/files/347.pdf (Accessed on 13.07.2010).

Rees, W. 2014. Avoiding Collapse: An agenda for sustainable degrowth and relocalizing the economy. British Columbia: Climate Justice Project, Canadian Centre for Public Policy Alternatives (CCPPA).

Reij, C., Tappan, G. and Smale, M. 2009. Re-Greening the Sahel- Farmer-led innovation in Burkina Faso and Niger. In: D. Spielman and R. Pandya-Lorch (eds.), Millions Fed. Washington D.C.: International Food Policy Research Institute (IFPRI), pp. 53-58.

Republic of Kenya. 2002. The Water Bill, 2002. Kenya Gazette Supplement, Bills 2002. Nairobi: Government Printer, Nairobi, pp. 287–413.

Republic of Kenya. 2007. Kenya Vision 2030. Available at: http://www.fao.org/fileadmin/user_upload/drought/docs/Vision%202030-%20Popular%20Version.pdf (Accessed on 13.05.2008)

Republic of Kenya. 2010. Water Sector Strategic Plan (WSSP) 2010-2015. Nairobi: Ministry of Water and Irrigation.

Roudi-Fahimi, F. Creel, L. and De Souza, R.M. 2002. Finding the balance: Population and Water Scarcity in the Middle East and North Africa. PRB MENA Policy Brief 2002. Washington, DC: Population Reference Bureau (PRB). Available at: http://www.prb.org/pdf/FindingTheBalance_Eng.pdf (Accessed on 05.04.2010).

Savenije, H.H.G., Hoekstra, A.Y. and van der Zaag, P. 2014. Evolving water science in the Anthropocene Hydrology and Earth System Sciences, 18: 319–332

Serageldin, I. 2012. Ismael Serageldin webpage. Available at: http://www.serageldin.com/Water.htm (Accessed on 07.09.2012).

Shiklomanov, I.A. 1993. Global fresh water resources. In: GLeick, P.H. (ed.), Water crisis: A guide to the freshwater resources, New York, Oxford University Press, pp. 13-24.

Shisanya, C.A. and Khayesi, M. 2007. How is climate change perceived in relation to other socio-economic and environmental threats in Nairobi, Kenya. Journal of Climate Change 85: 271-284.

Solomon, S. 2010. Water: The Epic Struggle For Wealth, Power, And Civilization'. New York, NY: HarperCollins Publishers.

The Water Project, Inc., US. 2016. Health and Water. Available at: https://thewaterproject.org/why-water/health (Accessed on 06.03.2017)

UNEP. [United Nations Environment Programme]. 2002. Global Environmental Outlook 3: Past, Present and Future Perspectives. Earthscan Publications Ltd: London. Available at: web.unep.org/geo/assessments/global-assessments/global-environment-outlook-3 (Accessed on 03.05.2013)

UNEP. [United Nations Environment Programme]. 2011. Towards a Green Economy: Pathways to Sustainable Development and Poverty Eradication. Available at: www.unep.org/greeneconomy (Accessed on 23.05.2012).

USGS. [United States Geological Survey]. 2016. Earth's water distribution Available at: http://ga.water.usgs.gov/edu/waterdistribution.html (Accessed on 10.11.2016)

WASREB. [Water Services Regulatory Board]. 2011. Financing Urban Water Services In: Kenya Utility Shadow Credit Ratings. Nairobi: Water and Sanitation Program (WSP).

WASREB. [Water Services Regulatory Board]. 2014. Assessing options to achieve commercial viability and financial sustainability of water supply and sanitation services. Nairobi: German Cooperation (GiZ).

Witcombe, C. 1999. H2O - The Mystery, Art, and Science of Water: Leonardo Da Vinci and Water. A Sweet Briar College Learning Resource — Spring Semester 1999. Available at: http://witcombe.sbc.edu/water/artleonardo.html (Accessed on 13.02.2013).

World Bank Group. 2016. High and Dry - Climate Change, Water, and the Economy. Water Global Practice. Washington, DC: International Bank for Reconstruction and Development, The World Bank. License: Creative Commons Attribution CC BY 3.0 IGO. Available at: www.worldbank.org (Accessed on 13.07.2012).

WSP. [Water and Sanitation Program]. 2012. Sustainable Services for Domestic Private Sector Participation Using Credit Ratings to Improve Water Utility Access to Market Finance in Sub-Saharan Africa. Washington: Water and Sanitation Program Briefing, February 2012.

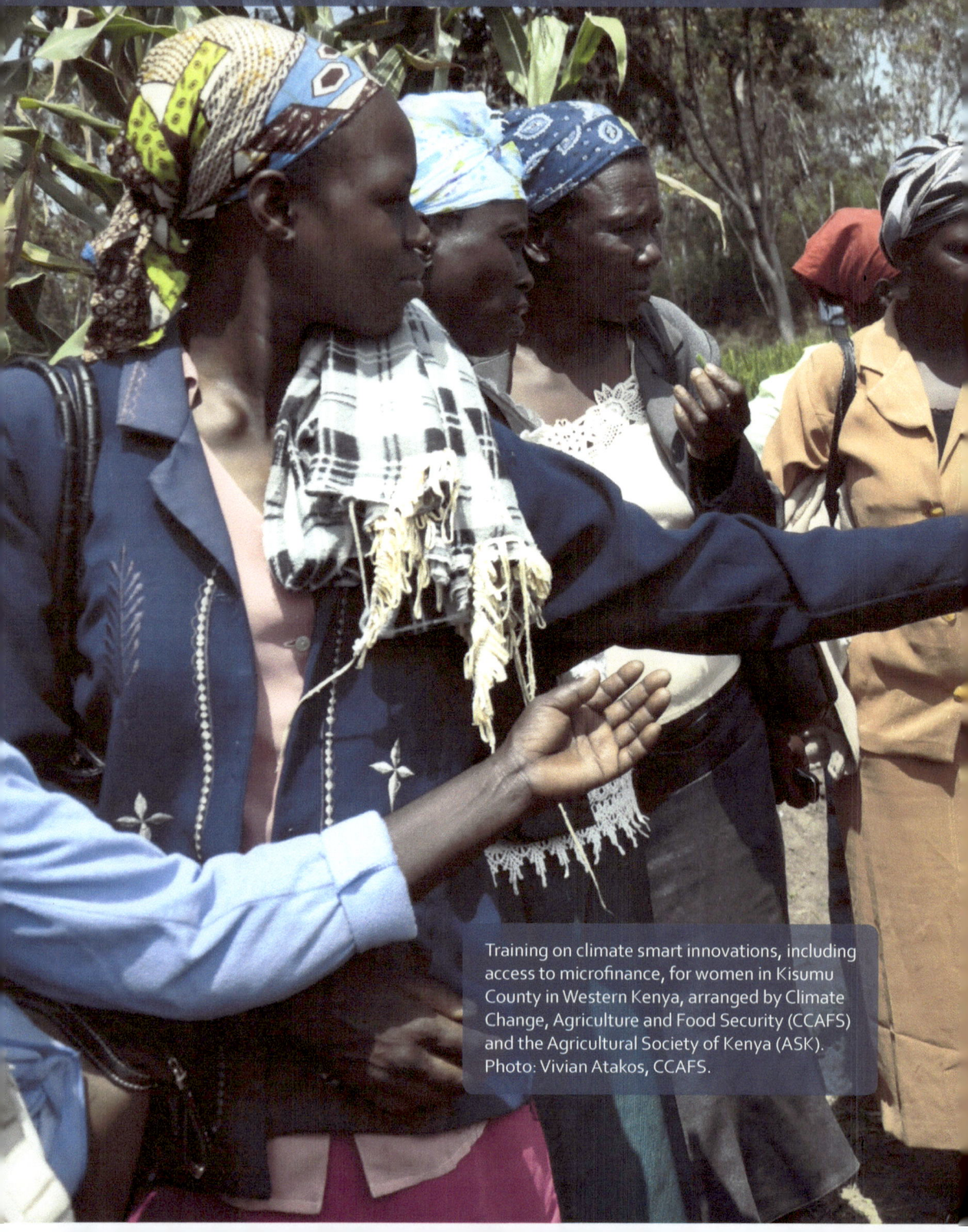

Training on climate smart innovations, including access to microfinance, for women in Kisumu County in Western Kenya, arranged by Climate Change, Agriculture and Food Security (CCAFS) and the Agricultural Society of Kenya (ASK). Photo: Vivian Atakos, CCAFS.

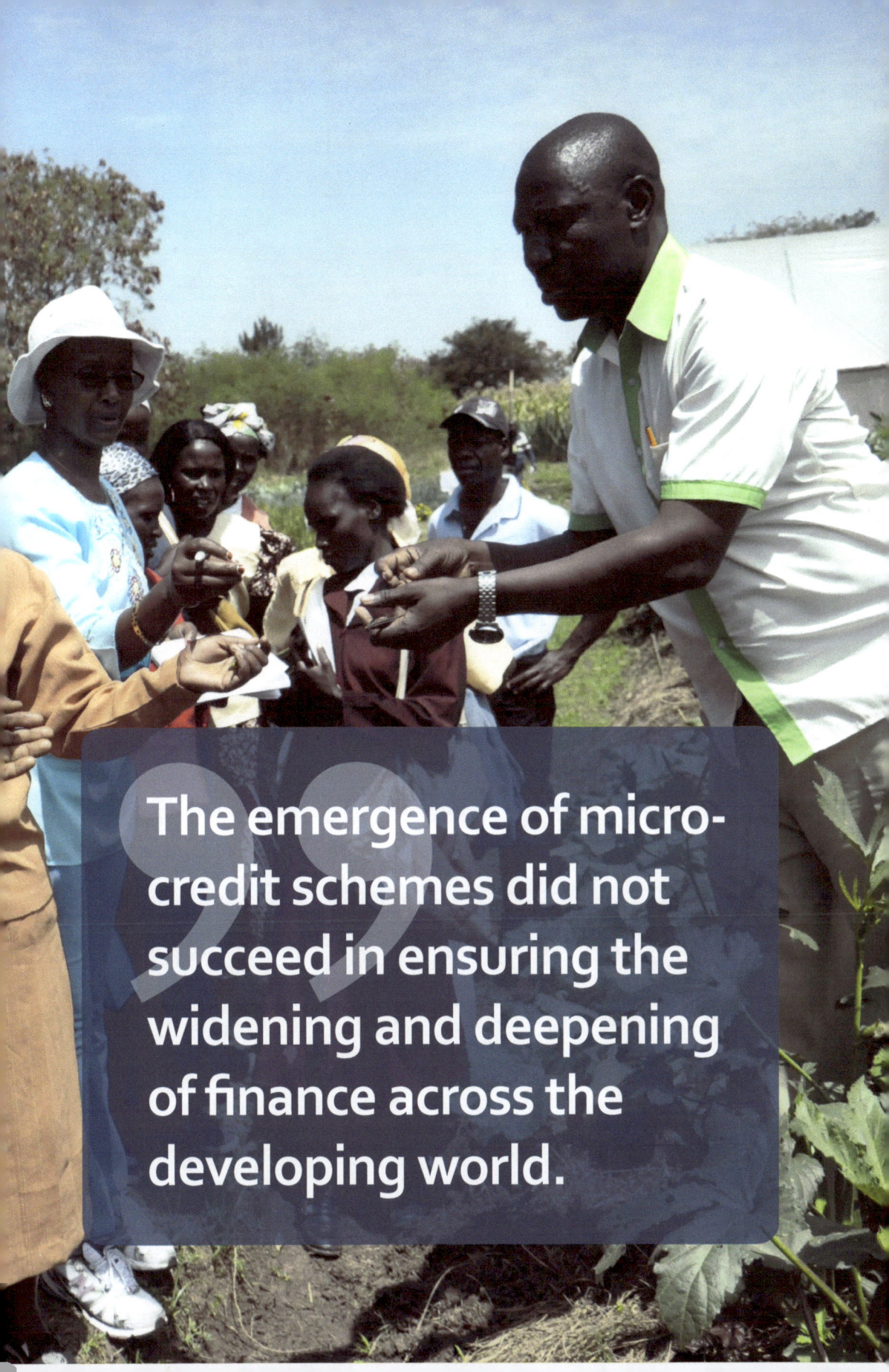

The emergence of micro-credit schemes did not succeed in ensuring the widening and deepening of finance across the developing world.

- WHETHER IN LOW-LATITUDE or mid-latitude climates, tropical economies are fragile by nature and vulnerable to climate change, dry weather and heat.
- Widespread rain-fed agriculture outstrips irrigated agricultural practices both in terms of scope and value-added, leading to low annual growth rates in food production
- THIS IS FURTHER AGGRAVATED by inadequate investments in human capital, agricultural infrastructure, and research and extension networks.
- BESIDES, RURAL WATER FINANCING faces sectoral rivalry and social exclusion for its perceived high risk due to reduced cashflows while resources are diminishing in a changing environment.
- THERE IS THUS a great need for rural water development in Africa and it deserves to be treated as indispensable as other social sectors in terms of human capacity enhancement, infrastructure development, research and extension service for improved farming systems and production technologies.
- ADDITIONAL RESOURCES must be mobilized, specifically to facilitate the management of water resources (including rainwater harvesting), promote irrigation and improve food security.
- THE COMPREHENSIVE AFRICA AGRICULTURE DEVELOPMENT PROGRAMME (CAADP), The Alliance for a Green Revolution in Africa (AGRA), the Millennium Challenge Account (MCA), and other programmes sponsored by bilateral and multilateral development institutions offer such assistance for the agricultural water development in Africa through direct transfer and the constitution of a sinking fund for microfinance and banking loans, and mostly for rain-fed agricultural activities.
- HOWEVER, MOST FARM HOUSEHOLDS receive less than what they ask for to finance their livelihood activities. This is of great concern, given that credit is among the critical factors that will drive Africa towards achieving its green revolution agenda.
- FINALLY, THE DEMAND for finance from rural households is shifting from for the agricultural sector to non-farming sectors, and thus makes it imperative to design and implement innovative financing mechanisms for the agricultural sector in general, and water in particular, if the sustainable development goals (SDGs) are to be achieved.These mechanisms could include microfinance schemes such as small credit financing and insurance mechanisms; the design and implementation of innovative contract arrangements between producers (or water service providers) collectives and market operators, as well as financial incentives for private service providers.

# Chapter 2:
# Africa's Water Sector Development and Financing Outlook

*Wangai Ndirangu, Cush Ngonzo Luwesi, Atakilte Beyene and Mamudu Abunga Akudugu*

## 2.1 Introduction

African states seek greater integration into the world's economy through farming, forestry, livestock keeping and aquaculture among other activities. The 55 countries that fall within the tropical and sub-tropical zones are currently working hard to achieve their sustainable development and poverty reduction goals (Figure 2.1).

Agriculture has always been the most important economic activity undertaken by Africans – from the primitive tribe up to the industrial society. It has been acknowledged as the engine of civilizations and economic development.[77] However, the famous Gourou Atlas (1953) reported that Africa's tropical environments were not as conducive to economic development as mid-latitude areas, on account of their hot climates, underutilized natural resources and the weak potential of their populations.[78] For Pierre Gourou, the unfavourable nature of the soil in low-latitude areas, of their potential photosynthesis, crop yields and food value chains, explained the poverty and fragility of their populations, and thus their underdevelopment.[79] Besides, the development of most of those areas was largely dependent on indigenous agriculture and unreliable food supply chains; unstable settlement; unsuitable conditions for stock raising; underutilization of natural resources; limitations of industrialization; and poverty.[80]

Even though Gourou and his followers to some extent exaggerated the intrinsic deficiencies of tropical environments, the disadvantages they suffer compared to mid-latitude areas cannot be denied or challenged in terms of potential photosynthesis, crop yields, health and poverty[81]. But with the changing global climates, even African mid-latitude climates of the north and the south are not spared by environmental externalities and poverty. For instance, the Southern Africa region is generally noted

---

77 Ellis, 1993
78 Mellinger, Sachs and Gallup, 2000
79 Clout, 2003
80 Ellis, 2006
81 Mellinger, Sachs and Gallup, 2000

for its high industrialization and its episodic dry spells, but it is facing uncommon development hardships due to water stranded assets. The record-setting drought of 2015–16 has resulted in enormous financial losses for water-related sectors, especially water supply, agriculture, energy, mining and related industries.[82] In South Africa alone, where the dry weather and heat is projected to last 23–24 months, there will be a loss of 30–40% of the country's 12 million tonne corn crop. Hence, South Africa will be forced to import 3–5 million tonnes of corn from other African countries to compensate for the loss, at a cost exceeding 15 billion Rand (i.e. $US 927 million). Yet, South Africa used to be an exporter of grain to southern African nations.[83]

## Type of climate

- Af: equatorial
- Am: monsoon
- Aw: tropical savanna

- BWh: warm desert
- Bwk: cold desert
- Bsh: warm semi-arid
- Bsk: cold semi-arid

- Csa: warm mediterranean
- Csb: temperate mediterranean

- Cwa: humid subtropical
- Cwb: humid subtropical/ subtropical oceanic highland
- Cwc: oceanic subpolar

- Cfa: warm oceanic/humid subtropical
- Cfb: temperate oceanic
- Cfc: cool oceanic

- Dsa: warm continental/mediterranean continental
- Dsb: temperate continental/mediterranean continental
- Dsc: cool continental
- Dsd: cold continental

- Dwa: warm continental/humid continental
- Dwb: temperate continental/humid continental
- Dwc: cool continental/subarctic
- Dwd: cold continental/subarctic

- Dfa: warm continental/humid continental
- Dfb: temperate continental/humid continental
- Dfc: cool continental/subarctic
- Dfd: cold continental/subarctic

- ET: tundra
- EF: ice cap

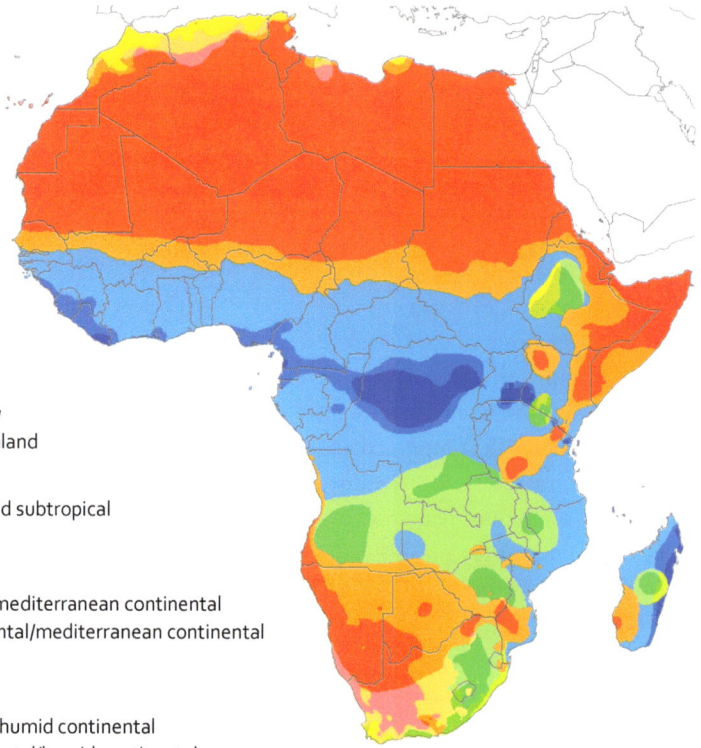

**Figure 2.1.** van Köppen Africa climate map [84]

82    Meservey, 2016
83    Sihlobo and Kapuya, 2016
84    Peel, and Finlayson and McMahon, T.A. 2007

Besides, it has been repeatedly emphasized that African resources have been underutilized – not so much in the sense of unemployment, but with regards to low value added and the inefficient and perverse allocation of the resources.[85] Moreover, the result of their reproductive behaviour has been a sustained population growth rate in most cases. The very high fertility rates versus a fairly high mortality has led to a high number and proportion of young dependants. These population patterns play a major role in dictating the state of the productive forces and the dependent nature of the development of most African countries.[86] With a per capita gross domestic product (GDP) that ranges from US$10,000 to less than US$100, agriculture accounts for more than 15% of GDP in most African countries, and especially in the poorest ones, where agriculture is the main source of income and employment.[87] Hence, there is a need for economies of scale to increase the economic efficiency of labour and the value added of natural resources to sustain economic development and enable future generations to benefit from the same resources.[88]

Ericksen (1998)[89] estimated that 69% of the fresh water available globally was utilized for food production, through irrigation. The remaining 31% was used for industrial production (23%) and domestic and administrative purposes (8%). Regarding the African continent, its share amounted to 88% for agriculture, 5% for industries and 7% for households and institutions. Thus, agriculture remains the most important water user and the biggest contributor to the social welfare and economic development of most African countries. However, due to the low level of technological development and the complexity of social behaviour, coupled with a variety of land covers and uses, as well as geologies, soil patterns, landforms, altitudes and climate, the availability of water leads to strikingly diverse agricultural patterns across Africa, from rain-fed agriculture to irrigation practices. However, widespread rain-fed agriculture outstrips irrigated agricultural practices both in terms of scope and value-added (Table 2.1).

It cannot be overemphasized that rain-fed agriculture remain the most important activity undertaken by Africans , with the exception of the Saharan and Kalaharian landscapes; but the types of crops and seeds vary widely across African countries. While population growth in Sub-Saharan Africa is increasing at an annual rate of 3%, food production is lagging behind at just 1–2% growth. The proportion of arable land irrigated in Africa in 2001 was around 5%, compared to 26% in other developing countries; meanwhile, fertilizer use was around 15 kg/hectare compared to 110 kg/hectare in other developing countries.[90]

---

85   Luwesi, 2010
86   Cleaver and Schreiber, 1992
87   Ellis, 2006
88   Brown, 2001
89   Ericksen, 1998
90   Chauvin, Mulangu and Porto, 2012

| Region | Rain-fed agriculture scope | Irrigated agriculture scope | Irrigated agriculture potential |
|---|---|---|---|
| Sub-Saharan Africa | Very high | Low | Very high |
| Middle East and North Africa | Low | Low | Very limited |
| Central Asia and Eastern Europe | Medium | High | Medium |
| South Asia | High | Very high | Medium |
| East Asia | High | Very high | Medium |
| Latin America | High | Medium | Medium |
| North America | High | Very high | Medium |
| OECD countries | Low | Medium | Medium |

Table 2.1. Regional characteristics of the global agricultural water outlook[91]

This situation is mainly due to land degradation, soil erosion, high yield losses caused by weeds, insects, economic and physical water scarcity, low use of inputs, climate change and related disasters. Furthermore, the increased prevalence of HIV/AIDS in the population has reduced labour availability and consequently farm productivity. This is further aggravated by inadequate investments in human capital, agricultural infrastructure, and research and extension networks. [92] Thence, the incidence of hunger and malnutrition across Africa is serious. To exploit the full potential of agricultural and rural development to reduce hunger and undernourishment in Africa, additional resources must be mobilized, specifically to facilitate the management of water resources (including rainwater harvesting), promote irrigation and improve food security.[93]

One specific case is that of Ghana. Its agriculture accounts for about a fifth (22%) of the country's GDP.[94] Indeed, the agriculture sector is the main source of livelihood for a large proportion of people resident in rural Ghana (and indeed Africa). Rural livelihoods are, however, currently strained due to the adverse effects of climate change. Crop yields continue to dwindle, as rainfall patterns are now unpredictable. There are instances of the double tragedy of drought and flood occurring in the same season. The experience of recent times has been either too much rain or too little, and both of these negatively affect agricultural production and rural livelihoods. This explains why farm households are not just the poorest in Ghana, but also contribute most to Ghana's poverty.[95] The situation is particularly dire in northern Ghana, which experiences unimodal rainfall patterns. A report by the Ghana Statistical Service (2014) shows that, although the level of extreme poverty is relatively low in Ghana, it is concentrated in rural savannah – largely northern Ghana, where more than a quarter of the people are

91 Adapted after van der Bliek, McCormick and Clarke, 2014
92 Gajigo and Lukoma, 2011; and Khan, 2001
93 Malesu, 2010
94 GSS, 2014
95 GSS, 2014

poor.[96] The key to escaping from this is to design and implement interventions, particularly irrigation, that ensure a stable water supply for production purposes.

## 2.2    Financing Agricultural Water Development in Africa: A Mere Dream?

The provision of irrigation facilities is strategic in rural areas, especially in arid and semi-arid lands (ASALs), where it is expected to help improve livelihoods. Thus small-, medium- and large-scale irrigation schemes have been provided in some of those areas to enhance agricultural production and encourage all-year crop production, which will ultimately lead to an improvement in livelihoods through increased food availability and income levels. Despite these decades-long concerted efforts to facilitate the development of rural livelihoods using irrigation as a strategic tool, there is still a high incidence of poverty in most African countries – and in particular in the ASALs.[97] The key reason for this is the lack of innovative financing mechanisms for irrigators to be able to take advantage of irrigation facilities. In areas with public-funded irrigation schemes, farmers still complain of inadequate access to productive resources allowing them to make efficient use of such irrigation facilities. There is a need to establish innovative financing arrangements for irrigated agriculture in ASALs. These could be equally applicable to irrigation financing in other situations across Africa and the developing world.[98]

Over the years, Africa's agriculture has relied on global financial support for its development. However, this support has not translated into key critical outcomes on the ground, especially in terms of the lives of smallholder farmers. Global agricultural support in Africa by development partners increased by about 66% between 2000 and 2010 in the cropping and livestock, forestry and fisheries subsectors, rising from US$7.5 billion to US$12.5 billion. This increase, however, was much lower in Sub-Saharan Africa (SSA) where it is reported to have risen from US$2.5 billion to about US$3.3 billion over the same period, which is about 30%.[99] What is more disturbing is that the need for global support to agriculture is greatest in SSA, but it recorded the lowest support in the agricultural water subsector – despite widespread recognition that increased investment in agricultural water development (AWD) is key to poverty reduction in the developing world.[100]

At the continental level, there have been some policy initiatives to improve the financing of smallholder farmers across Africa. African governments and their counterparts in industrialized countries – as well as bilateral and multilateral development institutions, such as the World Bank and the International Monetary Fund (IMF) –

---

96    GSS, 2014
97    MoFA, 2010
98    Akudugu, 2010
99    Stone, Agar, Carpio, Cabello and Hayes, 2012
100  Afrane, 2002

spearheaded these policy initiatives up until the 1980s and early 1990s.[101] The policies generally failed to deliver affordable finance in a sustainable way to smallholder farmers across the continent for a number of reasons, including political instability and bad economic management by governments. The failure of these policy initiatives, coupled with a deterioration in the economies of most countries of Africa in the 1980s, led to a paradigm shift towards economic recovery programmes (ERPs) and structural adjust-ment programmes (SAPs). As one of the conditions under SAPs, African countries were asked to liberalize their financial markets under the Financial Sector Adjustment Programme (FINSAP), which consequently led to the withdrawal of subsidies for ag-ricultural financing. The implementation of FINSAP therefore entirely changed the financial terrain and financial markets across Africa. The productive sectors then had to compete for finance allocation from the financial markets.[102] It is in such a context that a joint team from the World Bank and its partners met in June 2001 to discuss the promotion of AWD. Strategic plans for investment preparation were designed to revitalize interest in agricultural water investment in Sub-Saharan Africa. These dis-cussions, which later brought on board the New Partnership for Africa's Development (NEPAD) saw the development of a Comprehensive Africa Agriculture Development Programme (CAADP).[103] The latter gave an impetus to state members of the African Union to increase their investment in agricultural water within their national medi-um-term expenditure frameworks (MTEF).[104] Unfortunately, high risk is a characteris-tic feature of agriculture, which made it highly uncompetitive in the formal financial market. This accounts for the abysmal access to financial services, particularly credit, by smallholder farmers.[105]

## 2.3    Opportunities and Challenges for Financing a Green Revolution in Africa

Agricultural development triggered by green revolution has yet to take off in Sub-Sa-haran Africa in the way it did in Asia and Latin America in the 1970s, and much earlier in the industrial countries (Figure 2.2). Unlike other productive sectors – such as health and education, which deal largely with public goods – the actors in agricul-ture (including farmers, agribusinesses and service providers) are mainly private parties whose investments rely heavily on rainwater and to only a limited extent on agronomic technologies. Yet public investment is required especially for water and technology developments, which are necessary to build up a favourable environment for agricul-ture, even though private investors account for a large proportion of the required total

---

101  McKay and Aryeetey, 2004.
102  Agyeman-Duah, 2008
103  AGRA, 2009
104  World Bank, AfDB, FAO, IFAD and IWMI. 2008
105  Asante, Afari–Sefa and Sarpong, 2011

investment.[106] This is particularly so as traditional agricultural development support through public-driven projects has shown only limited capacity to achieve the desired impacts. Often their implementation is too rigid, and is neither market driven nor results based. It is therefore important to boost private investment in agriculture by building up an environment favourable to private investors, through the development of catalytic tools that provide incentives and alleviate the constraints on private investment.[107]

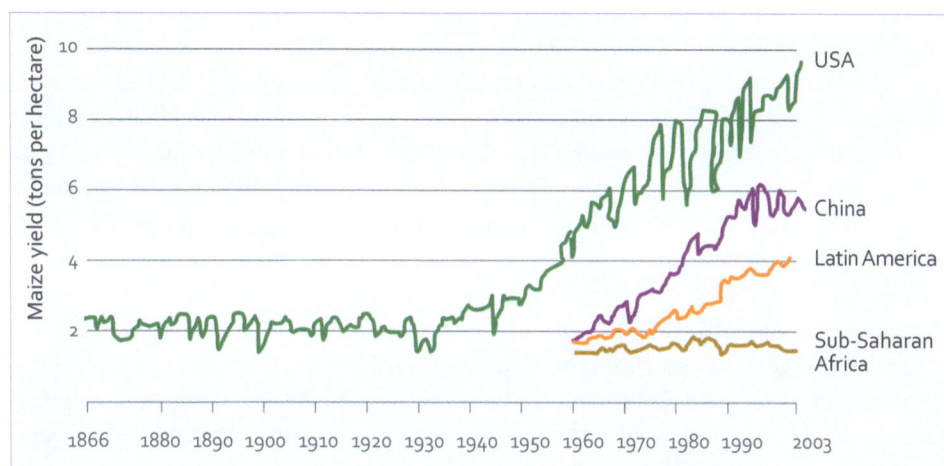

**Figure 2.2.** Sub-Saharan agriculture lagging behind the green revolution [108]

Nonetheless, in the wake of ERP, SAP and FINSAP, there emerge opportunities to address these agricultural financing challenges facing Africa. This can notably be done through microfinance institutions that specialized in the delivery of microcredit to poor households – especially in rural areas, where agriculture is the main livelihood activity. Most of the microfinance schemes designed as an alternative to mainstream bank lending employed the Grameen Bank approach of group lending.[109] The emergence of microfinance and microcredit schemes somehow did not succeed in ensuring the widening and deepening of finance across the developing world. As a result, the debate on the need to prioritize lending to the agricultural sector in the formal financial sectors across Africa resurfaced in the early 2000s. it led to the emergence of a number of interventions, including the Bill and Melinda Gates initiative dubbed Alliance for a Green Revolution in Africa (AGRA).[110] This offers another opportunity for a holistic resolution of the agricultural financing bottlenecks on the continent.

---

106  World Bank, AfDB, FAO, IFAD and IWMI, 2008
107  Stone, Agar, Carpio, Cabello and Hayes, 2012
108  Source: U.S. Data, U.S. Departement of Agriculture's National Agricultural Statistics; all other countries and regions, FAOStat. (van der Bliek, McCormick and Clarke, 2014)
109  de Aghion and Morduch, 2010
110   GRAIN Briefing, 2007

The overall objective of the AGRA initiative is to realize a food-secure and prosperous Africa through the promotion of rapid sustainable agricultural growth, based on smallholder farmers. The strategy is to make farming a business, rather than a way of life, as has been the practice, especially among smallholder farmers in Africa. One of the pillars of AGRA is to ensure that smallholder farmers have access to productive resources, including affordable finance, which constitutes a critical input. To put this into context, less than 1% of the available domestic private sector financing in Africa typically goes into agriculture. AGRA has developed a financial facility for smallholder farmers called the Innovative Financing Initiative (IFI).[111] The IFI aims to reduce the risks of lending to agriculture, by supporting commercial banks to design and deliver appropriate financial products to farmers. In AGRA's view, this will lead to improvement in the performance of agricultural markets and promote financial literacy among smallholder farmers. AGRA reports that it has kick-started a revolution in lending to small-scale farmers in Africa by using US$17 million to reduce the risks of lending facing banks . In collaboration with its partners, AGRA also reports leveraging US$160 million in affordable loans to farmers from commercial banks in Kenya, Tanzania, Ghana and Mozambique.[112]

Related to AGRA is the Millennium Challenge Account (MCA), sponsored by the United States government through its Millennium Development Authority (MiDA). The programme offers development assistance to selected African countries, including Ghana., Under this programme, the US government provided a total of US$547 million to Ghana from 15 February 2007 to 15 February 2012,. Following the successful completion of the five-year programme, the government of Ghana signed a new compact with the US government for a second phase of the project.[113] The first phase focused on smallholder farmers and their communities, with the overall goal of ensuring poverty reduction in the beneficiary communities through agricultural transformation, with an emphasis on three main areas – agriculture, transportation and rural development. In terms of agriculture, six key areas were targeted, with a total budgetary allocation of US$208.8 million. These included farmer enterprise training in commercial agriculture (US$62.13 million); development of irrigation facilities (US$24.8 million); land tenure facilitation (US$4.09 million); development of post-harvest infrastructure and value chain services (US$17.4million); agricultural credit provision (US$29.75 million); and construction of feeder roads (US$70.63 million).[114] The agricultural credit provision component of the programme was geared towards meeting the financial needs and alleviating the financial constraints of the 'unbanked' and 'under-banked' farmers in 30 of the 170-plus districts. The programme provided a revolving credit fund to 56 financial institutions for onward lending to farmers. These financial institutions included 11 commercial banks, 34 rural and community banks, 2 savings and loans companies and 9 financial NGOs. In all, some 10,506 borrowers engaged in far-

---

111  AGRA, 2009
112  AGRA, 2012
113  MiDA-Ghana, 2012
114  MiDA-Ghana, 2012

ming and related agricultural value chain activities benefited from the finance facility. Some US$16.74 million were disbursed to farmers and other actors in the agricultural value chain. Some funds were also allocated to training and capacity building in credit management and administration of the participating financial institutions. The aim was to ensure effective and efficient financial services delivery to the target clients. Nevertheless, there are issues over high default rates.[115]

At the national level, the need to improve access to credit in rural areas where most of the people reportedly depend on agriculture for their livelihoods has long been recognized in national agricultural investment plans (NAIPs) and policies across the nation states of Africa. For example, the government of Ghana produced the Medium Term Agriculture Sector Investment Plan (METASIP I & II) and the Food and Agriculture Sector Development Policy (FASDEP I & II).[116] The first phase of the policy (FASDEP I) was developed and implemented between 2006 and 2009. The second phase (FASDEP II) was implemented between 2010 and 2015. And the third phase is has been developed and is currently underway. The plan (METASIP I & II) and policy (FASDEP I & II) are based on the premise that access to financial services (particularly credit) by farm households is critical if they adopt improved farming systems and production technologies. This recognition underscores the importance of credit and other financial services in shaping the production behaviours of farmers. According to the Ministry of Food and Agriculture (2010), the promotion of access to finance by farmers and other actors along the agricultural value chain in Ghana is one of the key pillars of the policy (FASDEP I & II).[117] The obvious thing is that most of these financing initiatives place great emphasis on rain-fed agriculture at the expense of irrigated agriculture. Hardly any agricultural financing policies in Ghana have targeted irrigated agriculture. Interestingly, the returns on investment in irrigated agriculture far outweigh rain-fed production.

Regarding rural farming credits, the demands of formal and informal loans by farm households are largely not being met across Africa. Most households receive less than they ask for to finance their livelihood activities.[118] Borrowers who are considered poorlycreditworthy and who represent a high risk of default are 'rationed out' of the formal credit markets across Sub-Saharan Africa, especially in Ghana, Kenya and Nigeria.[119] Turvey et al. (2012) found that there is a heterogeneity factor in the credit demands of farm households which must be taken into consideration in developing tailor-made financial intermediations that are specific to the context of farmers and farm households across different regions of the world.[120] This is of great concern, given that credit is one of the critical factors that will drive Africa towards achieving its green revolution agenda, as captured in the AGRA framework.

---

115  MiDA-Ghana, 2012
116  MiDA-Ghana, 2012
117  MoFA, 2010
118  Zerai and Rani, 2012
119  Mwangi and Sichei, 2011
120  Turvey, He, Ma, Kong and Meagher, 2012

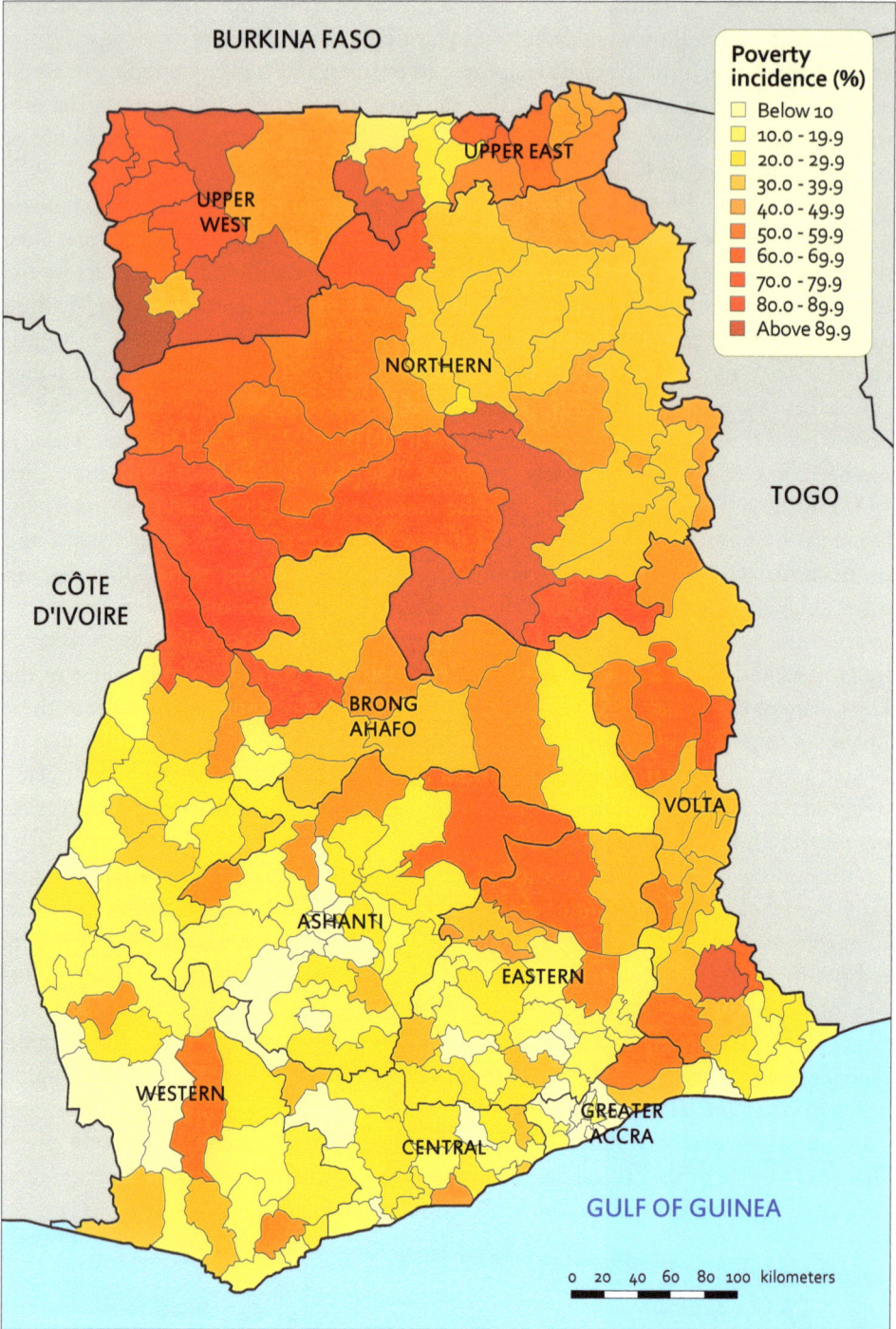

**Map 2.1. Incidence of poverty in Ghana.** Adapted from Ghana Statistical Service, GSS 2015.

Again, according to IFAD (2003), only 8% of small clients, particularly the poor in Ghana, for instance, are able to access financial services from the formal financial market.[121] As a corollary, about 92% of the poor mostly engaged in agriculture for livelihoods do not get credit from the formal credit market. This is worrisome, given that over two decades, various initiatives were launched in Ghana to ensure that poor people, particularly in the rural area, do get adequate access to formal credit and other financial services. Such policy initiatives include the establishment of rural and community banks and the liberalization of the financial market, Yet, after the implementation of these policy initiatives, widespread inadequate access to financial services (particularly credit) by rural households is reported across the country. The lack of access is severest among rural farm households in the poverty-endemic areas of the country, such as Upper West, Upper East and Northern Regions, which have poverty levels of 88%, 83% and 63%, respectively, against a national average of about 29%.[122] Only 21%, 19%, 14% and 11% of rural farm households in the Upper East, Upper West, Northern and North East Regions of Ghana, respectively, have access to formal financial services, particularly credit and savings facilities for their farming activities (i.e. primarily rain-fed and irrigated crop production, as well as animal rearing). At the national level, Demirgüç-Kunt and Klapper (2012) reported that only 20% of adult Ghanaians are included in the formal financial sector.[123]

While emphasizing the need for innovative financing for actors in the agricultural sector, particularly irrigation, it is important to recognize the growing non-agricultural sector in rural Africa. Thus, the role of livelihood diversification in agricultural financing is critical, as it shapes credit demand and supply dynamics. Many rural households that hitherto depended solely on agriculture for survival are now diversifying out of agriculture. This phenomenon has serious implications for the supply of finance to the agricultural sector.[124] Thus, the credit demand and supply dynamics has changed in rural areas, where until recently the main source of livelihood was agriculture. Indeed, the demand for finance from rural households is changing in favour of the non-farm sector. This makes it imperative to design and implement innovative financing mechanisms for the agricultural sector that take into consideration the diversified nature of rural livelihoods in recent times, with the non-farm sector becoming very important as a result of adaptation to climate change and climate variability.

## 2.4    What the Future Holds

There are good indications that private sector investment in agriculture and water in developing countries still lags far behind its potential. Some progress seems to have been made in recent years in Africa, following the Maputo Declaration of 2003; but

---

121  IFAD. 2003
122  GSS, 2008
123  Demirgüç-Kunt and Klapper, 2012
124  Akudugu, 2014

Photo credit AUC.

**Photo 2.1.** At the AU Summit in Malabo, Equatorial Guinea, in June 2014, the gathered heads of state adopted a declaration on accelerated agricultural growth. The 2014 Malabo Declaration upholds the 10 percent public spending target of the Maputo Declaration, adopted by the AU in 2003, which states that 10 percent of GDP should go to agricultural development.

it remains unsatisfactory in both size and scope. This is mainly due to tight economic and policy constraints, which make entrepreneurs and banks reluctant to invest in agriculture and water, as they are perceived to be associated with high climatic risk, which affects most African countries.[125] There is also the issue of price risk, due to the increased volatility of world food prices, the variability of water storage and local food production, and the lack of effective buffer storage mechanisms in most developing countries and particularly in Africa. Another issue of concern is the existence of counterpart risks, which is due to the difficulties associated with collaterals for credit in the traditional credit markets.[126] There are also a number of market failures, which prevent private investors from receiving the correct market signals, due largely to the lack of information, market rigidity and the high cost of entry. This calls for new and innovative financing mechanisms that address the above constraints. These mechanisms could include insurance schemes, design and implementation of innovative credit financing mechanisms, and innovative contract arrangements between producers or producer collectives and market operators, as well as innovative incentives for private service providers.[127] Innovative financing is essential if the sustainable development goals (SDGs) are to be achieved by the date set; this will be possible through agricultural sector-specific interventions. Lessons learned from the development and successful implementation of innovative financing mechanisms in other productive sectors could be used as an effective catalyst for private investment in the green development sector, agriculture and water included.

---

125  ONE.ORG/40Chances. 2013
126  Kibaara, 2006
127  Groobey, Pierce, Faber and Broome, 2010

# References

Afrane, S. 2002. Impact assessment of microfinance interventions in Ghana and South Africa: A synthesis of major impacts and lessons. *Journal of Microfinance* 4 (1): 41-57.

AGRA. [Alliance for a Green Revolution in Africa]. 2009. AGRA: Early Accomplishments, Foundation for Growth.

AGRA. [Alliance for a Green Revolution in Africa]. 2012 . Innovative financing initiative.

Agyeman-Duah, I. 2008. An economic history of Ghana: Reflections on a half-Century of challenges and progress. Oxfordshire: Ayebia Clarke Publishing Ltd.

Akroyd, S. and Smith, L. 2007. Review of public spending on agriculture: Main study and country case-studies, Joint DFID / World Bank study. Washington, D.C.: World Bank.

Akudugu, M. A. 2010. Assessment of access to financial capital by rural people in Ghana: The case of the Upper East Region. Savings and Development 34 (2): 169-189.

Akudugu, M. A. 2014. Farm credit and agricultural productivity in Ghana. Ph.D Thesis. Reading Berkshire: University of Reading.

Asante, B. O., Afari–Sefa, V. and Sarpong, D.B. 2011. Determinants of small scale farmers' decision to join farmer based organizations in Ghana. African Journal of Agricultural Research 6 (10): 2273-2279.

Brown, L.R. 2001. Eco-Economy: Building an Economy for the Earth. New York: W.W. Norton and Company Ltd.

Chauvin, N.D., Mulangu, F. and Porto, G. 2012. Food Production and Consumption Trends in Sub-Saharan Africa: Prospects for the for the transformation of the agricultural sector. UNDP WP 2012-011 (February 2012), UNDP Regional Bureau of Africa.

Cleaver, K.M. and Schreiber, G.A. 1992. The Population, Agriculture and Environment Nexus in Sub-Saharan Africa, Agriculture and Rural Development Series No. 1, Washington, D.C.: The World Bank, Technical Department-Africa Region,

Clout, H. 2003. The Géographie Universelle... but which Géographie Universelle ? Annales de Géographic, Vol. 112 (634): 563-582.

de Aghion, B.A. and Morduch, J. 2010. The economics of microfinance (2nd Edition). Cambridge, MA: Massachusetts Institute of Technology.

Demirgüç-Kunt, A. and Klapper, L. 2012. Financial inclusion in Africa: An Overview. World Bank Policy Research Working Paper WPS No. 6088.

Ellis, F. 1993. Peasant Economics: Farm Households and Agrarian Development. Cambridge: Cambridge University Press.

Ellis, F. 2006. Agrarian change and rising vulnerability in rural sub-Saharan Africa. New Political Economy 11 (3): 387-397

Ericksen, S.H. 1998. Shared river and Lake basins in Africa: Challenges for Cooperation". Ecopolicy, Series 10. Nairobi: ACTS English Press Ltd.

Gajigo, O. and Lukoma, A. 2011. Infrastructure and Agricultural Productivity in Africa. African Development Bank Market Brief 23 November 2011. Available at: https://www.afdb.org/fileadmin/uploads/afdb/Documents/Publications/ (Accessed on 13.10.2013)

GRAIN Briefing. 2007. A New Green Revolution for Africa?. November 2007 Issue. Available at: http://www.grain.org/briefings/ (Accessed on 13.07.2010).

Groobey, C., Pierce, J., Faber, M. and Broome, G. 2010. Finance Primer for Renewable Energy and Clean Tech Projects. Available at: http://www.wsgr.com/PDFSearch/ctp_guide.pdf. (Accessed on 05.05.2014).

GSS. [Ghana Statistical Service]. 2008. Ghana Living Standards Survey, Report Number 5. Accra: Government of Ghana publications.

GSS. [Ghana Statistical Service]. 2014. Ghana Living Standards Survey Round Six (GLSS 6). Accra: Government of Ghana publications.

GSS. [Ghana Statistical Service]. 2015. Ghana Poverty Mapping Report. May, 2015. Accra: Government of Ghana publications.

IFAD. [International Fund for Agricultural Development]. 2003. Ghana: Women's access to formal financial services. Available at: http://www.ifad.org/gender/learning/sector/finance/42.htm (Accessed on 16.04.2012).

Khan, M.H. 2001. Rural Poverty in Developing Countries Implications for Public Policy. International Monetary Fund (IMF) Current Issues No 26, March 2001. Available at: http://www.imf.org/external/pubs/ft/issues/issues26/ (Accessed on 06.03.2007)

Kibaara, B. 2006. Rural Financial Services in Kenya: What is Working and Why. Tegemeo Working paper (25)

Luwesi, C.N. 2010. Hydro-economic Inventory in a Changing Environment – An assessment of the efficiency of farming water demand under fluctuating rainfall regimes in semi-arid lands of South-East Kenya. Saarbrüken: Lambert Academic Publishing.

Malesu, R.M. 2010. Strategies for increasing agricultural water productivity in physically and economically water.scarce regions of ACP. In: CTA Annual Seminar 2010- Closing the Knowledge Gap: Integrated Water Management for Sustainable Agriculture. Wageningen: The ACP-EU Technical Centre for Agricultural and Rural Cooperation (CTA), pp 3-4. Available at: http://annualseminar2010.cta.int (Accessed on 13.10.2013)

McKay, A. and Aryeetey, E. 2004. Operationalizing pro-poor growth: A country case study on Ghana. A joint initiative of AFD, BMZ (GTZ, KfW), DFID, and the World Bank. Available at: http://www.dfid.gov.uk/pubs/files/oppgghana.pdf.%3E (Accessed on 24.10.2011).

Mellinger, A.D., Sachs, J.D. and Gallup. J.L. 2000. Climate, Coastal Proximity, and Development. In : L.C. Gordon, M.P. Feldman and M.S. Gertler (Eds.), The Oxford Handbook of Economic Geography. Oxford: Oxford University Press, pp. 169-194. Available at: http://www.univpgri-palembang.ac.id/perpus-fkip/Perpustakaan/East%20Phylosopy/Economic%20Geography/Economic%20Geography,%20Oxford%20Handbook.pdf (Accessed on 08.11.2007)

Meservey, J. 2016. Record-Setting Drought in Africa Requires U.S. Leadership onDisaster Relief. The Heritage Foundation ISSUE BRIEF No. 4556 ( May 4, 2016). Available at: http://report.heritage.org/ib4556 (Accessed on 06.03.2017)

MiDA-Ghana. [Millennium Development Authority]. 2012. MiDA Meet The Press – CEO's Speech. Available at: Retrieved from http://mida.gov.gh/site/?p=4316 (Accessed on 12.02.2012).

Millennium Development Authority (MiDA)-Ghana. 2012. op.cit.

MoFA. [Ministry of Food and Agriculture]. 2010. Ghana Medium Term Agricultural Sector Investment Plan (METASIP). Accra: Government of Ghana publications.

Mwangi, I.W. and Sichei M.M. 2011. Determinants of access to credit by individuals in Kenya: A comparative analysis of the Kenya National FinAccess Surveys of 2006 and 2009. European Journal of Business and Management 3 (3): 206-226.

ONE.ORG/40Chances. 2013. The Maputo Commitments and the 2014 African Union Year of Agriculture. Available at: https://s3.amazonaws.com/one.org/images/131008_ONE_Maputo_FINAL.pdf (Accessed on 21. 01.2015).

Peel, M.C., Finlayson, B.L. and McMahon, T.A. 2007. Updated world map of the Köppen-Geiger climate classification. Hydrol. Earth Syst. Sci. 11: 1633-1644.

Sihlobo, W. and Kapuya, T. 2016. Will Southern Africa cope with the current drought? Available at: http://www.grainsa.co.za/will-southern-africa-cope-with-the-current-drought (Accessed on 06.03.2017)

Stone, R., Agar, J., Carpio, A., Cabello, M. and Hayes, J. 2012. Study of African and international innovations and best practices in increasing access to rural and agricultural finance. Oxford: Oxford Policy Management and Kadale Consultants Ltd. Available at: http://www.opml.co.uk/sites/default/files/Agrifinance-innovations-final-report.pdf (Accessed on 13.10.2013)

Turvey, C.G., He, G., Ma, J., Kong, R. and Meagher, P. 2012. Farm credit and credit demand elasticities in Shaanxi and Gansu. China Economic Review 23 (4): 1020-1035.

UNDP. [United Nations Development Programme]. 2012. Transformation of the Agricultural Sector. UNDP Africa WP 2012-011 (February 2012). Available at: http://www.undp.org/content/dam/rba/docs/Working%20Papers/Food%20Production%20and%20Consumption.pdf (Accessed on 13.10.2013)

van der Bliek, J., McCormick, P. and Clarke, J. 2014.On target for people and planet: Setting and achieving water related sustainable development goals. Colombo: IWMI [International Water Management Institute].

World Bank, AfDB, FAO, IFAD and IWMI. 2008. Investment in Agricultural Water for Poverty Reduction and Economic Growth in Sub-Saharan Africa – A Synthesis Report. Washington, D.C.: The World Bank.

Zerai, B. and Rani, L. 2012. Is there a tradeoff between outreach and sustainability of microfinance institutions? Evidence from Indian Microfinance Institutions (MFIs). European Journal of Business and Management 4 (2): 90-98.

Water users tend to assume that natural resources are 'free gifts from God', available at all places and at all times.

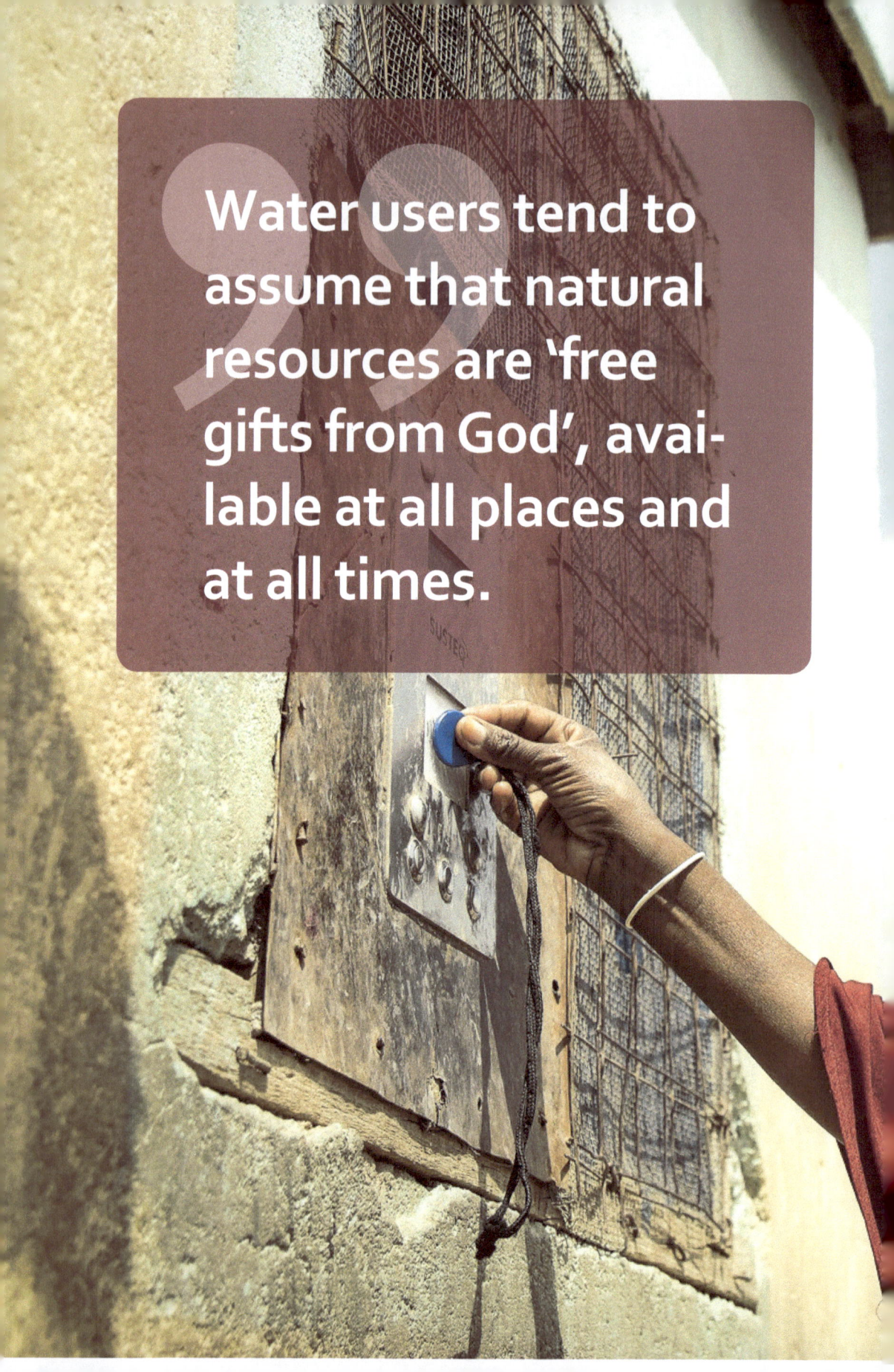

# 3. The Core Business of Integrated Water Management: Achieving Water Governance Performance

Arron Gesar, 34, holds her token to collect water from a water ATM in Hadado, Kenya. These ATMs help communities to fight drought. Photo credit Katie G Nelson, Oxfam.

- WITH THE GLOBAL CLIMATE CHANGE and population growth, major river basins and lakes are continuously being degraded. Thus, water management involves interventions on both the container of water (i.e. the 'watershed' or 'catchment area') and the watershed content (i.e. 'water resources').
- WATER RESOURCES CANNOT be managed in a vacuum, but only in its natural, political, institutional, socio-cultural, economic and technological environments, within the watershed boundaries.
- WATER GOVERNANCE PERFORMANCE (WGP) is a major goal toward achieving sustainability in integrated water resources management (IWRM) through accountability, efficiency and responsiveness.
- WGP INTERMEDIATE DEVELOPMENT OUTCOMES (IDOs) include enhanced transparency and oversight of the public administration system, which leads to increased protection of the watershed and the safe reproduction of ecological systems, the renewal of the hydrological cycle, efficient and equitable distribution of resources, and finally to environmental sustainability.
- THE FULL PARTICIPATION of all stakeholders, including women and disabled people, in the planning, implementation, management, decision-making and monitoring and evaluation of watershed interventions is the basis for good governance.
- WOMEN MUST BE EMPOWERED to take effective part in decision- making at all levels of watershed management, but not only for providing water at the household level and being custodians of water sources. They should also play a key role in sharing the benefits resulting from the utilization of water.
- PUBLIC INVOLVEMENT IN WATERSHED MANAGEMENT is essential for maintaining the catchment area and ensuring the sustainability of water provision and related sanitation services delivery by private businesses.
- RESEARCHERS SHOULD COORDINATE efforts towards implementing the 'user/polluter pays' principle, raising complex issues leading to resource scarcity and eliciting water economic value to enable greater willingness to pay and resource use efficiency.
- THERE IS FINALLY A NEED for political will to enable IWRM champions to arrange for adapted policies and strategies, regulatory and institutional frameworks, as well as management tools, technological, financial and economic instruments.
- WITH SUCH A CONDUCIVE ENVIRONMENT, water managers are likely to access public funding (taxes, tariffs and transfer), as well as build adequate infrastructure for service delivery through public-private partnerships in the watershed.

Chapter 3:

# The Core Business of Integrated Water Management: Achieving Water Governance Performance

*Joy Apiyo Obando, Cush Ngonzo Luwesi, Atakilte Beyene,*
*Raphael Mwamba Tshimanga and Albert Ruhakana*

## 3.1    Introduction

When people ask for water, we wonder whether we should bring the container (i.e. the 'cup') or the content (i.e. 'water'). To save time and money, the bearer should consider bringing not only the water, in sufficient quantity and of decent quality, but also an appropriate container (e.g. a cup). That is why water management involves the planning and programming, implementation and coordination, monitoring and evaluation (M&E) of interventions related to both the container of water (i.e. the 'watershed' or 'catchment area') and the watershed content (i.e. 'water resources').

This is crucial, because water as a resource cannot just be transported and served up in a vacuum (like radio and television waves). Besides, with the global climate change and population growth, major river basins and lakes are continuously being degraded. Since this unique structural container keeps not only water, but also other resources on which the catchment's development depends, a water crisis poses serious problems of other resources provision and availability, leading to new development challenges. The management of water resources thus lies at the heart of the Sustainable Development Goals (SDGs) number 6 and 8.[128]

Figure 3.1. Goals 6 and 8 of the altogether 17 Sustainable Development Goals (SDGs), also known as Agenda 2030, set by the United Nations in 2015.

---

128  IUCN, 2016 and SIWI, 2016

In Sub-Saharan Africa, most countries were unable to supply adequately clean water for them to meet the Millennium Development Goals (MDGs) on access to water and sanitation services by 2015.[129] The concept of 'integrated water resources management' (IWRM) was designed to develop a framework that would help water managers to understand the complexity of the watershed and to achieve three major goals in the management of this precious liquid: economic efficiency, social equity and environmental sustainability (Figure 3.2). These goals translate into the core business of IWRM, which is to achieve water governance performance (WGP).

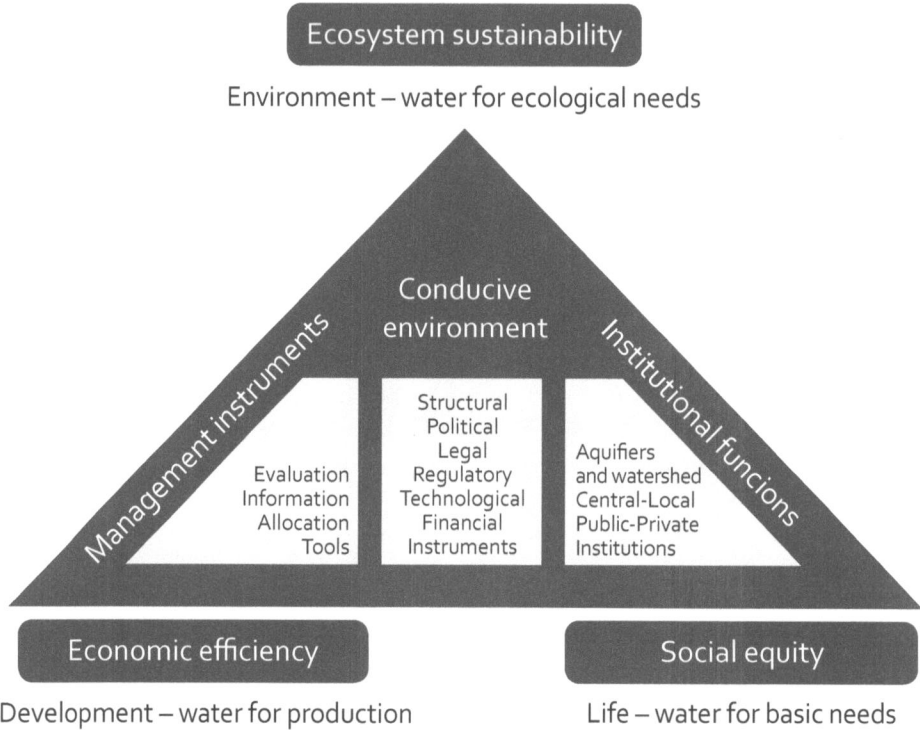

Figure 3.2. Integrating sector interests, goals and outcomes within the IWRM framework [130]

## 3.2    Concept of Integrated Water Resources Management

Bearing in mind the three cornerstone goals of IWRM, the Global Water Partnership (GWP)[131] provides a broad definition of 'integrated water resources management': 'a process that promotes the coordinated development and management of water, land and related resources, in order to maximize the resultant economic and social welfare

129  UN, 2016
130  GWP, 2000
131  GWP, 2000

in an equitable manner without compromising the sustainability of vital ecosystems'. This means that IWRM recognizes the interdependency between water subsectors, related resources, biological systems and the ecosystems on which they depend, to ensure its sustainability. It also integrates all types of water users and key stakeholders in the management and development of water resources for equitable distribution of the resource. Finally, IWRM promotes water resources as an economic asset, by integrating all costs incurred by competing users and the interests of interdependent sectors within the same framework to achieve efficiency (Box 3.2).

| Low | Partial | High |
|---|---|---|
| Mono-sectoral view: focus on water as resource (with attention to externalities) | Focus on water and another resource sector (with attention to externalities) | Focus on water and multiple other resources (with attention to externalities) |
| • Integrated management of water quantity and water quality aspects in particular water courses<br>• Ensuring the conjunctive use of groundwater and surface water resources | • Land and water management in irrigation<br>• Waste water reuse in agriculture<br>• Enforcement of minimum river flow for the protection of agro-ecological landscapes | • Integrated resources management in a watershed<br>• River basin management<br>• Various control measures for ecosystems protection and services, notably water storage and supply |
| EU-Water – Framework Directive (IHE-Definition) | CGIAR-WLE – IWRM for Agriculture (IWMI & FAO Definition) | GWP – IWRM Definition IUCN Ecosystems Based Approach |

**Box 3.2.** Degree of Intersector Integration [132]

The nexus between water, land, food and energy is well elicited in the definitions of IWRM by the European Union (EU), the Global Water Partnership (GWP), the International Union for Conservation of Nature (IUCN), The UN Food and Agriculture Organization (FAO) and the Water, Land and Ecosystems (WLE) programme of the Consultative Group for International Agricultural Research (CGIAR) being implemented by the International Water Management Institute (IWMI). The EU treats water as a natural resource meant for human consumption, while the GWP and IUCN focus on the watershed (or catchment area) as a reservoir of natural resources and as a natural ecosystem, respectively. The UN/FAO and the CGIAR/WLE consider water as a natural ecosystem service specifically designed for agricultural production (see Box 3.2).133 Hence, Jaspers (2001) suggests that, in order to coordinate all these sectoral

---

132 Adapted from Förch, Winnegge and Thiemann, 2005
133 van der Bliek, McCormick and Clarke, 2014 and Merrey, Drechsel, de Vries and Sally, 2005

interests, goals and outcomes, IWRM should operate within a holistic framework that captures: (i) all waters (spatial management); (ii) all interests (social management); (iii) all stakeholders (participatory management); (iv) all levels (administrative management); (v) all relevant disciplines (technological management); and (vi) sustainability in all senses: environmental, political, social, cultural, economic, financial and legal (organizational management). This would definitely lead to better performance in water governance. To achieve WGP, water sector actors and managers need to design the necessary processes and operations. Their performance may simply be measured in quantity of fresh water and related services yielded over a certain period of time and space to the satisfaction of all users. A fixed unit quantity is generally recommended to measure performance, since the hydrological cycle cannot simply be adjusted to yield any quantity of water to meet increasing human development needs. There is also a need for coordinated efforts between socio-economic development and the protection of natural ecosystems in the watershed, as per the first principle of the 1992 Dublin Conference.

In terms of processes and operations, achieving WGP requires accountability, efficiency and responsiveness. Accountability calls for clarity of roles in the legislative and executive processes. Efficiency involves higher outputs to be obtained at a lower cost for the utilization of environmental, social, political and economic resources. Responsiveness necessitates policies that are bound to clear objectives and an evaluation of future impact and, where available, of past experience, in order to deliver what is needed in terms of demand. Each institution must explain and take responsibility for what it does and how it does it.[134] Such implementation of the concept of IWRM is expected to result in good governance, coupled with effectiveness, accessibility and equity, as well as sustainability in the long run.

## 3.3    WGP Intermediate Development Outcomes (IDOs)

The first IDOs expected from WGP operations and processes are enhanced transparency and oversight of the public administration system in the watershed in the short and medium terms. This results in increased protection of the watershed for the safe reproduction of ecological systems and renewal of the hydrological cycle, which in turn leads to environmental sustainability.

> **» Fresh water is a finite and vulnerable resource, essential to sustain life, development and the environment «**
>
> ICWE, 1992 – Dublin Principle 1

WGP is also expected to provide: (i) an economic value for water and other related resources; (ii) efficiency for water use in agriculture and other productive uses of water; (iii) effectiveness in the delivery of watershed infrastructure and services;

---

134  Hoff, 2011

and (iv) enhanced accessibility and equity in the distribution of public services, management roles and water resources across ages, genders, social classes, locations, etc. Table 3.1 clearly summarizes the operations and processes related to WGP.

| Type of intervention | Targets | Actions to be taken |
|---|---|---|
| Political Management | Political framework | Setting objectives for the use, protection and conservation of water resources |
| | Legal framework | Enacting rules needed for implementation of the political framework and attainment of its objectives |
| | Financing structures | Mobilizing and allocating financial resources to satisfy water needs and develop water resources |
| Institutional Management | Organizational framework | Creating an organ that will be able to coordinate all formal and functional aspects of IWRM |
| | Institutional capacity building | Developing human resources |
| Management Instruments | Water resources evaluation | Accounting for available resources versus needs |
| | Development of IWRM plans | Assorting and aggregating different options for development and utilization of water resources along with human interaction |
| | Demand management | Using efficiently the available water resources |
| | Social change | Building a water-friendly civil society |
| | Conflict resolution | Managing disputes through equitable sharing of water |
| | Regulatory instruments | Setting limits for water distribution and use |
| | Economic instruments | Utilizing water value and price to achieve efficiency and equity |
| | Information sharing and management | Improving knowledge of water resources for their better management |

**Table 3.1.** Areas of water governance performance[135]

135  Cap-Net, 2008

## 3.4 Opportunities and Challenges for Achieving WGP on the Ground

Achieving all the different IWRM objectives and outcomes has become very challenging in terms of implementation on the ground. In order to put the concept into practice, there is a need for multidisciplinary efforts to be made in the social and natural science and engineering fields to generate integrated scientific methods and approaches, including the new ICT tools that rapidly tackle some of the most complex and expanding water, land and ecosystem issues. Research in this area has seen considerable changes and developments over recent years. Research into issues such as hydrological modelling, the engineering of irrigation systems, land and soil erosion, as well as the distribution and species composition of ecosystems has continued, with an emphasis on increasing productivity and sustainability. Recent developments have seen increased demand for social, economic and environmental trade-offs to be minimized while intensifying productive activities in the watershed. Even though IWRM has been widely adopted and applied on the international and regional scales, it has yielded few or no tangible results in most developing countries. Moreover, different countries in the same region tackle the challenges of meeting their water needs differently, according to their own circumstances and development priorities, with no consideration for the transboundary nature of their water catchments.

Paradoxically as it may seem, the IWRM concept has been criticized for being more like a metaphysical belief than a pragmatic paradigm that inspires water politics and management practices. The concept is so broad as to have no real meaning, on the one hand, and on the other hand, so narrow that it focuses mainly on water without linking it directly to land and livelihoods management, said some critics. Others maintained that IWRM takes insufficient account of the politics that are at the core of most important water-related decisions.

Molle (2008) concludes that there is often a pretence that all these different objectives behind IWRM can be maximized simultaneously, whereas in reality only a balance can be achieved. There will always be trade-offs, either temporally (i.e. present versus future consumption) or spatially (i.e. in terms of land use or allocation of water for food production, energy generation or anything else). In the context of IWRM, trade-offs arise from management and utilization choices made by users or managers, which can change the type, magnitude, quality and relative mix of ecosystems services provided by the watershed. This finally results in an 'opportunity cost' of a choice, the 'cost' of an alternative forgone in exchange for something else.

In this regard, the food, energy, water (FEW) nexus approach has some merit, but it has also attracted criticism for being unnecessarily limiting and prescriptive. The FEW nexus approach for implementing IWRM is mainly criticized for not explicitly highlighting inter-linkages with climate change, poverty and pro-poor development. It has worked quite well at the river-basin level in a number of places. Following its successes recorded in North America, India and East Africa, some researchers have invested in the development of a 'light IWRM' concept, also referred to as 'integrated watershed management' (IWM), to maximize the contribution of IWRM to Sustainable Development Goals and to minimize conflict among stakeholders.

This light IWRM or IWM involves a process of regulating, planning and managing human activities and natural resources based in the watershed, which is the smallest hydro-ecological system that is manageable. This approach allows the protection of important water resources, while addressing simultaneously critical issues of human development and climate change impacts. Watershed management thus implies prudent use of the resources – such as land, soil, water, biodiversity and biomass – in a watershed for optimum productivity with minimal disruption to the environment. Bamutaze et al. (2014) define IWM as follows:

> Integrated Watershed Management is a holistic and integrated approach for sustainable management of a watershed area ... Integrated Watershed Management is a process of rational decision making in successive steps. Systematically the available management options are compared, and a Watershed Management Plan is developed that is mainly a rural development concept.

This integration of all target resources in the management aims to address tradeoffs and minimize the potential negative impacts of the actions of one particular subsector or group of stakeholders over a period of time on others. It seeks to avoid the inefficiencies and conflicts that feature the less-integrated approaches of IWRM decried earlier. In contrast to the prescriptive top-down IWRM integration, IWM aims to be problem focused, opportunistic and adaptive/iterative when applying the core principles of IWRM, especially at the water-user level. The intended outcome of applying IWM is a system of regulating, planning and managing water resources and water services delivery that is better adapted or tailored to the political economy of a given area.

## 3.5 Stakeholder Participation for Performance in Water Management

It should be noted that IWM places emphasis on the principle of public participation, to ensure inclusiveness and create interactions between the public and private sectors and with civil society, people of different genders and generations, urban locations and rural areas, in order to achieve a sustainable management of water resources, as put forward by the Dublin Principles 2 and 3.

These principles imply that where water is a matter of concern, everyone is a stakeholder and has his/her vested interests that must be taken into account. Thus, IWM values and promotes gender mainstreaming and intergenerational equity to build strong partnerships in catchment management. A good example is offered by the provisions in the constitutions of most water users' associations. Even in a male-dominant cultural setting, women are expected to account for at least 50% of the management of the associations. This recognition of the key role of women in the custody of water resources has led to the improvement of many catchment areas. Increasingly the IWM approach is being implemented across Africa.

IWM thus implies a move away from the traditional subsector approach of addressing domestic water supply, wastewater, irrigation, industry and the environment separately (often within different agencies or government departments) to the more holistic approach of water resources development and management to address problems that affect both the very local river basin and specific water-user communities by drawing on a wide range of stakeholders.

» Water development and management should be based on a participatory approach, involving users, planners and policy-makers at all levels «

ICWE, 1992 – Dublin Principle 2

With IWRM-specific country strategies and plans, successes from small watersheds can be transferred to tackle problems in wider river basins and in locations of national and regional significance.[136] Nonetheless, implementing the IWM approach on a larger scale remains a challenge, especially when it comes to intersectoral coordination and the integration of small watershed management programmes within the national action planning process, which involves bottom-up action plans. Even so, IWRM requires the full

» Women play a central part in the provision, management and safeguarding of water «

ICWE, 1992 – Dublin Principle 3

participation of local stakeholders in the management of water resources, if performance is to be achieved at a national or regional level.[137] True participation can only take place if all members of the national community come together to express their choices concerning water leaders, decide on the use of the catchment area and the allocation of water and other resources without compromising the needs of the future generations. They should also take part in the management process leading to the protection and conservation of these scarce resources in the watershed (Box 3.3).

» Water has an economic value in all its competing uses and should be recognized as an economic good as well as a social good «

ICWE, 1992 – Dublin Principle 4

In the same vein, women are expected not only to raise their voices, but also to take the lead among community members, as per the third principle of the 1992 Dublin Conference.

---

136  Jensen, 2013
137  ICWE, 1992

Women are not only well known for providing water at the household level, but also for being custodians of water sources. They also play a key role in collecting and safeguarding water for agricultural use.[138] Yet, when it comes to sharing the benefits, they are often left aside, or are simply 'kicked out' of management.[139] That must change; they need to be empowered to take effective part in decision-making at all levels of watershed management (Table 3.2).

## Effective participation

Real participation occurs only when stakeholders are actually part of the decision-making process. However, there are determinants, conditions and challenges related to participation in most countries.

**Determinants of the types of participation and conditions for effective participation**
- The type of participation depends on the spatial scale (river basin or village water system) relevant to the particular water management and investment decision.
- The nature of the political environment in which decisions take place.

**Challenges to the participatory approach**
Participation does not always achieve consensus as the following challenges reveal:
- Arbitration processes and other conflict resolution mechanisms are sometimes needed.
- Government intervention is sometimes needed to create an enabling environment for marginalised social groups such as the poor, indigenous people, the elderly, and women.
- Opportunities for participation are insufficient to provide the gains of the participatory approach. Currently, disadvantaged groups must also have the capacity to participate. Capacity building to enhance participation of disadvantaged groups is important.

**Box 3.3.** Determinants, conditions for effective participation, and challenges. Source: Cap-Net, 2006.

| Level of Participation | Planning and Decision-Making Process |
|---|---|
| Local Level | Domestic water use planning, management and M&E |
| | *e.g. providing and using water resources subject to operational rules, to meet existing demands and needs on an operational level* |
| Regional Level | River basin management |
| | *e.g. supply and demand management within a region, allocating water flows in a water district, ecosystem maintenance within a watershed* |
| (Supra) National Level | Water policy and legislation |
| | *e.g. national/supranational strategy for integrated water resources management* |

**Table 3.2.** Different scales of participatory watershed management.

---

138  OECD, 2016
139  Joshi, and Fawcett, 2006

## 3.6 Mainstreaming Economic Valuation for Sustainable Water Financing

Participatory watershed management should involve all users, suppliers, political leaders, water researchers and development partners. All stakeholders should agree on the value of their water resource in all its competing uses.[140] By improving water valuation, water researchers should explain to the community the causes of, and remedies for, water scarcity, in order to facilitate decision-making. They should demonstrate the 'economic value of water in all its competing uses', as recommended by the Dublin Principle 4.[141] Otherwise, IWRM will miss its core business, which is the performance management of water resources and services.

Ignorance of the full economic potential of water leads to the failure of IWRM. If misconceptions about the value of water persist, maximum benefit from water resources cannot be derived.[142] Watershed managers are thus required to place a value on water resources, so as to ensure its sustainability into the future. Otherwise, future generations would not have access to potable water and sanitation at an affordable price.[143] This, however, does not mean putting the fundamental human right of universal access to water on the back burner; rather it is an incentive and precautionary measure for good management and sustainability of this limited resource.[144] Why?

First of all, consensus is needed between all actors interested in water and watershed development, starting with the smallest level of water governance – a watershed – in accordance with the *principle of hydro-solidarity*.[145] This principle states that a river basin should be considered in its entirety as a whole physical unit, irrespective of political and administrative boundaries.[146] A watershed is not an administrative entity and does not depend on resources belonging to a particular administration alone. Thus, water governance should take account of different watershed components and their interactions, which make the watershed a unique entity with appropriate resources.[147] These include the hydrosphere (surface and ground waters), the troposphere (soils), lithosphere (rocks), biosphere (living creatures) and atmosphere (mainly the mass of gases surrounding the Earth– in interaction with the sun's energy – that determine the climates on the surface).[148] Besides, IWRM takes care of water quality and quantity in the management of disasters to address issues of wildlife habitat, livestock grazing, pollution prevention, land development, vegetation management and water supply.[149] For that reason, *ecosystem valuation* would greatly assist watershed managers and local

---

140  Calizaya, Meixner, Bengstoon, and Berndtsson, 2010.
141  GWP, 2000
142  Harrison and Qureshi, 2000
143  Luwesi, 2010
144  OECD, 2011
145  Gerlak, 2009
146  Falkenmark and Folke, 2002
147  IWA, 2003
148  Sendama and Granit, 2002
149  Turton, 2001

Photo Credit: IWRM AIO SIDS

*Mauritius, 29 January 2016.* Man drilling piezometric boreholes to assess groundwater quality and locate sources of contamination. His work is part of an Integrated Water Resources Management (IWRM) project, implemented by the United Nations Development Programme (UNDP), for Small Island Developing States in the Atlantic and Indian Oceans (SIDS-AIO). By helping to ensure availability and sustainable management of water and sanitation for all, the project feeds into the 2030 Agenda (SDG 6).

stakeholders, including diverse agencies, landowners, resource managers and non-governmental organizations, to coordinate their efforts and cooperate in implementing the *'user/polluter pays'* principle to solve these complex issues.[150] By recognizing the economic value of natural resources, they will be able to generate better results and save money in the long run through adequate planning and decision-making.[151]

Finally, water users tend to assume that natural resources are 'free gifts from God', available at all places and at all times. However, when these resources become scarce, users are ready to pay for – them as for any other commodity or service that they value; the more their willingness to pay, the higher their resource use efficiency.[152] Hence, integrating the economics of natural resources into consumer behaviour change provides a basis for the valuation of water resources and services (Table 3.3).[153]

---

150  Turner and Daily, 2008.
151  Shisanya, Luwesi and Obando, 2014
152  van Zyl, Store and Leiman, 2000
153  Harris, 2008

| Categories of Ecosystem Services | Ecosystem Benefits (Services/ Goods) | Beneficiary Activities | Expected Outcomes |
|---|---|---|---|
| **Provisioning Services** | Food (fodder) | Gathering and agriculture (agro-industry, crop and livestock management, fisheries and agro-business) | Direct/indirect utilization for subsistence, value addition and economic development |
| | Fresh water for drinking Fresh water for non-drinking purposes | Health (nutrition and sanitation) Waste/food/materials processing/ recycling Other Industrial uses | Healthy and potable water availability for drinking, washing-up, cleansing and restitution of pollutants |
| | Raw materials (fibre, timber) | Forestry and related industrial processes and businesses | Income generation, value addition and economic development |
| | Genetic resources | Biogenetics | Lifecycle maintenance/habitat and gene pool |
| | Bio-chemicals Biomass and energy resources  Ornamental resources | Biochemistry/pharmacy Biomass/wood processing  Arts/construction | Good health Power generation  Gardening/sheltering Beautification/aesthetics |
| **Regulating Services** | Air quality regulation | Recreational industries/tourism | Healthy and clean environment to support life and recreation/ tourism |
| | Purification of water and related ecosystems | Environmental management | Healthy and clean environment Pollution prevention, purification of waste, toxics and other nuisances |
| | Water flows/quality regulation | Maritime transport Water treatment Disaster management | Maintenance of water conditions for navigation, recreation/tourism Flood/drought prevention and moderation of other extreme events |
| | Erosion prevention  Climate/Pest/ Disease regulation | Health, nutrition and sanitation Environmental management | Good health for living in a clean environment Environmental protection |
| **Support services** | Carbon/nitrogen/water cycles  Soil formation  Pollination | Gathering and agriculture (agro-industry, crop and livestock management, fisheries and agro-business)  All other fields | Primary production of nutrients  Maintenance of soil fertility  Lifecycle maintenance/habitat and gene pool  Environmental protection |
| **Cultural services** | Knowledge systems/ educational values | Scientific and educational systems | Intellectual inventions/ innovations |
| | Spiritual/emblematic representations, moral/ religious values | Faith-based/occult organizations' activities (churches, mosques, temples, magic, divination practices...) | Spiritual, artistic and cultural diversity |
| | Aesthetic values | Space management  Aesthetic, plastic/martial arts, painting, music, choreography | Representational interactions  Income generation, value addition and economic development |
| | Recreation and ecotourism | Recreational industries and tourism | Idem |
| | Other cultural outputs (existence, bequest) | Other cultural activities | Idem |

**Table 3.3.** Direct and indirect benefits accrue from water and related ecosystems services [154]

154 MEA, 2005

Developing a taxpayer-driven administrative culture is highly recommended to enable behaviour change in favour of implementation of IWRM. However, strategic organizational and administrative changes should follow people's willingness and should take account of what they want. They should facilitate that process, rather than create barriers and obstacles to people's willingness to pay. In an effort to demonstrate the economic value of water in rural areas policy- and decision-makers should coordinate water abstractions for competing uses, public as well as private. This would lead water users to optimize their use efficiency in the whole catchment area.

In the context of water conservation, there are several issues involving *Payment for Environmental Services (PES)* and the sustainable use of water resources. Managers should bear in mind that drought ('too little' water), flood ('too much' water) and pollution ('too dirty' water) are three categories of stress resulting in extra costs for water management.[155] They increase the opportunity costs of water shortage, saving and treatment, respectively. Without a fair price being paid to cover the expenses related to restoring water quality and quantity, water managers would not be able to respond to high water demands for irrigation and food production, hydropower generation and industrial uses – a demand driven by steady population and economic growth.[156] Moreover, the high variability in the available water resource – due to the impact of pollution, environmental degradation and climate change – will likely lead to water crises, because of the lack of adequate infrastructure, technologies and competences to maintain and conserve water.[157] This will result in an increased risk of failure of socio-economic activities, owing to insufficient funds being available to clean and channel water for domestic and industrial consumption, as well as for the purposes of sanitation.

> » Three categories of water stress that would be exacerbated by climate change:
> (i) Too little
> (ii) Too much
> (iii) Too dirty «
>
> Kundzewicz, 2007

## 3.7 Improving Institutional Frameworks and Tools for Sustainable Water Financing

To achieve IWRM performance targets, water managers should create a conducive environment for water development and management. This involves political and legal frameworks to enable a national policy and strategy that is to be enacted in water

---

155 Hattingh, Turton, Colvin, Claassen, Ashton and Godfrey, 2007
156 Ayoo and Horbulyk, 2008
157 OECD, 2002, and Mohayidin, Attari, Sadeghi and Hussein, 2009

rules (laws and regulations). Thereafter, the rules should be translated into institutional frameworks that define the key actors and their roles within clear organizational structures (Table 3.4).[158]

| Enabling environment | Institutions | Management |
|---|---|---|
| **Laws and policies** | **Roles and responsibilities** | **Structures to** |
| • Frame water resources management within a country and between countries | • Of basin and other water sector organisations at different levels in the government, non-government and private sectors | • Assess water resources (availability and demand) |
| **Water user dialogues** | • Effective co-ordination mechanisms | • Set up communication and information systems |
| • Cross-sectoral and upstream -downstream dialogues | • Planning process | • Resolve conflicts in allocation of water |
| • Basin committee | • Financing | • Establish regulations |
| **Budgets** | | • Establish financing arrangements |
| • Financing organisations and investment | | • Establish self-regulation (voluntary actions) |
| **Co-operation** | | • Research and develop |
| • Within international river basins | | • Undertake development works |
| | | • Ensure accountability |
| | | • Develop organisational capacity |
| | | • Co-ordinate |

Table 3.4. The three dimensions of water management frameworks.[159]

Appropriate instruments for water resources and services delivery should be designed during the planning process, the implementation, and monitoring and evaluation to enable social change, conflict resolution, infrastructure development for resource allocation and related services provision. Then, innovative financing and economic instruments will add to this arsenal of management tools. The GWP has developed a comprehensive element toolbox containing a wide range of knowledge experience and instruments used in the water sector.[160]

If the desired environment for catchment management has not yet been established, it would be difficult to raise the necessary funding for water development. There would be a great need for 'champions' to foster water sector reforms in the spirit of IWRM. These are opinion leaders, researchers, policy-makers and institutions interested in ensuring water governance and financing, so that water is available for people and productive activities. These champions are keen on the protection of vital ecosys-

---

158  GWP and INBO, 2009
159  GWP and INBO, 2009
160  GWP, 2005

tems (or ecological capital) and the rational management of the spatial and temporal variability of water, as well as of the risks related to disaster, particularly in the course of climate change.[161] IWRM champions are expected to create awareness, sensitize public opinion and induce the political will for behaviour change to 'ease access to water, the efficiency with which resources are used, the capacity of people to benefit, and the health of the environment', which determine what is known as 'water security'.[162] Champions will doubtlessly contribute to well-planned and well-administered watersheds and seek the necessary funding for water development. This will require them to influence political leaders and their partners to take deliberate decisions to invest in water infrastructure; to manage, maintain and conserve water resources; and to allocate equitably the benefits from water development across various subsectors of the economy.

With such a conducive environment, watershed managers will be able to access public funding, namely: taxes, tariffs (in the form of charges, tariffs and fees) and transfers (the '3Ts'). All funds have to come from a combination of these sources. Water businesses may take the risks of raising further repayable types of finance, particularly bank loans and microfinance. Large water facilities may also raise bond and equity finance, usually with the backing of the government.[163] These public-private partnerships are likely to emerge as innovative financing mechanisms, to enable the building of large infrastructure, such as multipurpose dams and large irrigation schemes.[164] Lastly, funds will have to be channelled through the designated institutional frameworks to allow for accountability and transparency. This will ensure that adequate infrastructure and services are delivered, and that the watershed is conserved in the desired state.

---

161  Mukhtarov and Cherp, 2014
162  Clarke and King, 2004
163  GWP and INBO, 2009
164  Bidwell and Ryan, 2006

# References

Alemu, B. and Kidane, D. 2015. Rainwater harvesting: An optiuon for dry land agriculture in the arid and semi-arid Ethiopia. *Int. J. Water Res. Eng.* Vol. 7(2): 17-28.

Ayoo, C.A. and Horbulyk, T.M. 2008. The potential and promise of water pricing. Journal of International Affairs 61(2): 91-104.

Bamutaze, Y., Thiemann, S. and Förch, G. 2014. Integrated Watershed Management- A Tool for Urban Water Security. Workshop Results from Mbale, Uganda. Mbale: Makerere University, IWM Expert GmbH and FreieUniversität Berlin

Bidwell, R.D. and Ryan, C.M. 2006. Collaborative Partnership Design: The Implications of Organizational Affiliation for Watershed Partnerships. Society and Natural Resources 19 (9): 827-843.

Biswas, A.K. 2004. Integrated water resources management: A reassessment. *Water International*, 29, 248–256.

Calizaya, A., Meixner, O., Bengstoon, L. and Berndtsson, R. 2010. Multi-criteria decision analysis (MCDA) for integrated water resources management (IWRM) in the lake Poopo basin, Bolivia. Water Resource Management 24:2267–2289.

Cap-Net. [Capacity Development in Sustainable Water Management]. 2008. Economics in sustainable water management, Training manual and facilitators guide. available at: http://cap-net.org/sites/capnet.org/files/Economics%20of%20water%20FINAL.doc (accessed on 11.09.2011).

Clarke, R. and King, J. 2004. The Atlas of Water. Mapping the world's most critical resource. London: Earthscan.

Falkenmark, M. and Folke, C. 2002. The ethics of socio-ecohydrological catchment management: Towards hydrosolidarity. Hydrology and earth Systems Science 6 (1): 1–9.

Förch, G., Winnegge, R. and Thiemann, S. 2005. DAAD Alumni Summer School 2005: Topics of Integrated Water Resources Management. Weiterbilding in Siegen (18): 1-180.

Gerlak, A.K., Varady, R.G. and Haverland, A.C. (2009). Hydrosolidarity and International Water Governance. International Negotiation, 14: 311–328.

GWP. [Global Water Partnership] and INBO. [International Network of Basin Organizations]. 2009. A Handbook for Integrated Water Resources Management in Basins. Stockholm: Elanders.

GWP. [Global Water Partnership]. 2000. Integrated Water Resources Management. Technical Advisory Committee (TAC) Paper No 4. Stockholm: Elanders.

GWP. [Global Water Partnership]. 2005. IWRM Toolbox. Available at: http://www.gwp.org/global/toolbox/about/toolbox/toolbox%20(english).pdf Accessed on 12.07.2007)

GWP. [Global Water Partnership]. 2015. Integrated Water Resources Management in Eastern Africa: Coping with 'Complex Hydrology'. In Technical Focus Papers (TFP) No 7. Stockholm: Elanders.

Harris, J.M. 2008. Ecological Macroeconomics: Consumption, Investment and Climate Change. GDAE Working Paper No. 08-02. Available online at URL: http://www.ase.tufts.edu/gdae/ pubs/ wp/08-02EcologMacroEconJuly08.pdf (Accessed on 13.07.2012).

Harrison, S.R. and Qureshi, M.E. 2000. Choice of stakeholder groups and members in multi-criteria decision models. Nat Resour Forum 24:11–19.

Hattingh, H., Turton, A., Colvin, C., Claassen, M., Ashton, P. and Godfrey, L. 2007. Water and Water Pollution, Overview. CSIR. Available at: http://www.enviropaedia.com/topic/default.php?topic_id=240 (accessed on 09.11. 2013).

Hoff, H. 2011. Understanding the Nexus. Background Paper for the Bonn2011 Conference: The Water, Energy and Food Security Nexus. Stockholm: Stockholm Environment Institute (SEI).

I2iE. [International Institute for Water and Environmental Engineering]. 2010. Technical manual for the integrated water resources management. Ouagadougou: Groupe EIER-ETSHER. Available at: www.2ie-edu.org (accessed on11.09.2011).

ICWE. [International Conference on Water and the Environment]. 1992. The Dublin Statement on Water and Sustainable Development. Dublin: Secretariat of the International Conference on Water and the Environment.

IUCN. [International Union for Conservation of Nature]. 2016. Knowledge for SDG Action in West Asia and North Africa: R-KNOW Water Governance Best Practices within the Water, Energy,Food and Climate Change Nexus. Amman: IUCN- Regional Office for West Asia. Available at: www.iucn.org/westasia (Accessed on 06.03.2017)

IWA. [International Water Association]. 2003. Workshop 6 (Synthesis): "Water for efficient, sustainable fisheries and aquaculture." Water Science and Technology 51, 8: 155.

Jensen, K.M. 2013. Viewpoint–swimming against the Current: Questioning development policy and practice. Water Alternatives, 6, 276–283.

Joshi, D. and Fawcett, B. 2006. Water projects and women's empowerment. Available at: https://assets.publishing.service.gov.uk/media/57a08d67ed915d3cfd0019f6/R65752.pdf (Accessed on 13.07.2010).

Kazbekov, J., Abdullaev, I., Manthrithilake, H., Qureshi, A. and Jumaboev, K. 2009. Evaluating planning and delivery performance of water user associations (WUA) in Osh Province, Kyrgyzstan. Agricultural water management 96: 1259-1267.

Krumme, K. 2006. EFU - Ecological Functional Units: A Basis for Sustainable Development Planning.In: Förch, G., Winnegge, R. and Thiemann, S. (eds.), DAAD Alumni Summer School 2006: Participatory Water Resources Management Plan, FWU Water Resource Publications (5): 17-28.

Lenton, R. and Muller, M. 2009. Integrated water resources management in practice. Better water management for development. London: Earthscan.

Luwesi, C.N. 2010. Hydro-economic Inventory in a Changing Environment – An assessment of the efficiency of farming water demand under fluctuating rainfall regimes in semi-arid lands of South-East Kenya. Saarbrüken: Lambert Academic Publishing.

MEA. [Millennium Ecosystem Assessment]. 2005. Ecosystems and Human Well-being: Synthesis. Washington, DC.: World Resources Institute (WRI), Island Press.

Meire, P., Coenen, M., Lombardo, C. and Robba, M. 2008. Integrated Water Management - Practical Experiences and Case Studies. Dordrecht : Springer.

Merrey, D.J., Drechsel, de Vries, P.F. and Sally, H. 2005. Integrating "livelihoods" into integrated water resources management: taking the integration paradigm to its logical next step for developing countries.Regional Environmental Change, 5: 197–204

Mohayidin, G., Attari, J., Sadeghi, A. and Hussein, M.A. 2009. Review of water pricing theories and related models. African Journal of Agricultural Research, 4 (13): 1536-1544.

Molle, F. 2008. Nirvana concepts, narratives and policy models: Insight from the water sector. Water Alternatives, 1 (1): 131-156.

Moriarty, P., Butterworth, J. and Batchelor, C. 2004. Integrated water resources management and the domestic water and sanitation sub-sector. Thematic Overview Paper. Delft: IRC [International Water and Sanitation Centre].

Mukhtarov, F. and Cherp, A. 2014. The hegemony of integrated water resources management as a global water discourse. In: V.R Squires, H.M. Milner and K.A. Daniell (Eds), River basin management in the twenty-first century: Understanding people and place. Boca Raton: CRC Press, pp. 3-21.

OECD. [Organisation for Economic Co-operation and Development]. 2011. Together for Better Public Services: Partnering with Citizens and Civil Society, OECD Public Governance Reviews. Paris: OECD Publishing. Available at: http://dx.doi. org/10.1787/9789264118843-en (accessed on 29.03.2016).

OECD. [Organisation for Economic Co-operation and Development]. 2016. The Synthesis Report of Target 1 Stakeholders' Engagement for Effective Water Policy and Management. In Proceedings of the 6th World Water Forum, Marseille, 12–17 March 2012. Available at: http://www.worldwaterforum6.org/uploads/tx_amswwf/CS1.1__Stakeholder__s_engagement_for_effective_water_policy_and_management_Report.pdf (accessed on 09.11.2016).

OECD. [Organisation for Economic Co-operation and Development]. 2002. Social issues in the provision and pricing of water services. Paris: OECD.

Perrone, D. and Hornberger, G. 2014. Water, food, and energy security: scrambling for resources or solutions? Wiley Interdisciplinary Reviews: Water, Vol. 1 (1): 49–68.

Savenije, H.H.G. and van der Zaag, P. 2002. Water as an economic good and demand management, paradigms with pitfalls. Water International 27 (1), 98-104.

Savenije, H.H.G., Hoekstra, A.Y. and van der Zaag, P. 2014. Evolving water science in the anthropocene. Hydrology and Earth System Sciences, 18:319–332

Sendama, A. and Granit, J. A. 2002. New Approach to the Joint Management of River Basins in the Lake Victoria Basin – Nile Equatorial Subsidiary Action Program Proceedings Balancing Human Security and Ecological Security Interests in a Catchment-Towards Upstream/Downstream Hydrosolidarity. Proceedings of the 2002 SIWI Seminar. Stockholm: Stockholm International Water Institute (SIWI).

Shah, T. and van Koppen, B. 2006. Is India ripe for integrated water resources management IWRM: Fitting water policy to national development context. Economic and Political Weekly XLI (31): 3413-3421.

Shisanya, CA., Luwesi, CN. and Obando, JA. 2014. Innovative but Not Feasible: Green Water Saving Schemes at the Crossroad in Semi-Arid Lands. In: P. Chanie (eds.), Innovative Water Resource Use and Management for Poverty Reduction in Sub-Saharan Africa: An Anthology. Addis Ababa: OSSREA, pp. 137-172.

SIWI. [Stockholm International Water Institute]. 2016. 2016 World Water Week: Water for Sustainable Growth – Overarching Conclusions. Available at: http://www.worldwaterweek.org/wp-content/uploads/2016/10/2016-Overarching-conclusions-web-2.pdf (Accesssed on 06.03.2017)

Turner, R. and Daily, G. 2008. The ecosystem services framework and natural capital conservation, Environ Resour Econ, 39 (1): 25-35.

Turton, A. 2001. Towards Hydrosolidarity: Moving From Resource Capture to Cooperation and Alliances. Keynote Address for the 2001 SIWI Seminar. Stockholm: SIWI [Stockholm International Water Institute].

Tussupova, K., Berndtsson, R., Bramryd, T. and Beisenova, R. 2015. Investigating Willingness to Pay to Improve Water Supply Services: Application of Contingent Valuation Method. Water Resources Engineering & Center for Middle Eastern Studies, Lund University. Water 7: 3024-3039.

UN. [United Nations]. 2016. Sustainable Development Goals. Available at: http://www.un.org/sustainabledevelopment/development-agenda/(Accessed on 29.03.2016).

van der Bliek J., McCormick, P. and Clarke, J. 2014. On target for people and planet: Setting and achieving water related sustainable development goals. Colombo: International Water Management Institute (IWMI).

Van Zyl, H., Store, T. and Leiman, A. 2000. Measuring the costs of rainforest conservation in Cameroon. In: J. Reitbergen-McCracken and H. Abaza (eds.), Environmental Valuation: A Worldwide Compendium of Case Studies. London: Earthscan Publications Ltd, pp. 64-77.

Nairobi, July 2016. Willy Bett (left), Cabinet Secretary of Kenya's Ministry of Agriculture, Livestock and Fisheries, greets UN Secretary-General Ban Ki-moon upon his arrival for the UN Conference on Trade and Development (UNCTAD). Photo: Rick Bajornas, UN.

Development partners' donations, grants and loans represented almost a third of the total funding of the water sector.

# CHAPTER 4

# Summary

- THE STEADY GROWTH of water demands, climate change impacts and other environmental trends threaten water security in many parts of the world.
- TRADITIONAL SOURCES of financing present many constraints for water sector development, thus the need for visionary policies and legislation to harness water security through local investments in water and sanitation services, as well as through the conservation of catchment areas.
- THESE REFORMS are desperately needed in Africa, not only for the provision of essential water services, but also for the operationalization of the legal and institutional frameworks that guide the administration of the water sector and to keep finances flowing to the sector by ring-fencing the water sector revenues, good governance, organizational competence, financial management and budgetary discipline.
- IN GENERAL, a far-reaching rationalization of sectoral operations is introduced to: (1) bring the various subsectors under one ministry in charge of water management and development; (2) separate the management of water resources from the provision of water services; (3) de-link policy-making from day-to-day administration and regulation; (4) devolve some administrative functions to the lower level of the state governance structure; and (5) involve non-government entities in the management of water resources, as well as in the provision of water services.
- THESE REFORMS are expected to improve managerial capacities, abilities and performance to deliver quality services that are affordable to all, while ensuring efficiency and cost recovery in daily business. This should attract financing from development partners to achieve the SDGs of eradicating poverty, illiteracy and disease.
- AFRICAN GOVERNMENTS also need to provide a stable macroeconomic framework, reliable financial legislation, adequate economic policies and effective communication strategies to stimulate innovative thinking and risk-taking in the water sector.
- GOVERNMENTS SHOULD ENSURE political and public confidence, and provide incentives to private investors for funding the water and sanitation services.
- PARTNERSHIPS WITH THE PRIVATE SECTOR can best fill the gap of the 3Ts (tariffs, taxes and transfers) and severe budgetary pressure created by government reluctance to subsidize tariffs of water services or guarantee borrowing.
- TO ATTRACT MORE innovative finances, especially those in commercial form, all water and sanitation services (WSS) should enhance their creditworthiness and capacity to take commensurate risks by such means as: (1) designing, preparing and submitting bankable projects to lenders; (2) enhancing good governance and the ability to manage debt within their structures; (3) introducing a culture of record-keeping through the accounting and auditing of finances; (4) increasing demonstrated cashflow to sustain cost recovery and the repayment of loans; and (5) taking specific measures to deliver services to the poor and socially excluded through the funding of small-scale WSS projects.
- A WATER SECTOR INVESTMENT PLAN is needed to guide the sector toward achieving the national economic vision of a middle-income country.

Chapter 4:

# Legal and Market Requirements for Water Finance in Africa: The Kenya Water Sector Reforms Case

*Pauline Matu Mureithi, Cush Ngonzo Luwesi, Mary Nyawira Mutiso, Nele Förch and Amos Yesutanbul Nkpeebo*

## 4.1   Introduction

The world water resources will be the major casualties of global warming. Kundzewicz et al. (2007) noted that 'There are three categories of water stress that would be exacerbated by climate change: (i) Too little; (ii) Too much; and (iii) Too dirty' water.[165] Hulme et al. (2001) predicted increased precipitations in most arid and semi-arid lands (ASALs) of Africa during dry periods.[166] Yet these and certain humid areas suffer from lower precipitations during almost the whole year. Therefore, they need visionary policies and legislation to harness water security through local investments in water and sanitation services, as well as the conservation of catchment areas.[167]

Water services providers (WSPs) and their resource manager counterparts across Africa experience serious problems in expanding their coverage and in providing reliable services to consumers. Their most notable problems are limited management capacity, low operating revenues and lack of access to long-term finance.[168] Public funds to improve these systems are largely absent, but only a few of these resources are allocated to the development of new water sources and systems in very low-income areas with poor access to water.[169] For that reason, many African governments have initiated several reforms in the water sector to curb the decreasing water investment trend and give room to water development.[170] The Republic of Kenya, which is our model case in this book, started a reform in 1999, which climaxed with the release of the Water Act

---

165  Kundzewicz, Mata, Arnell, Doll, Kabat, Jimenez, ... Shiklomanov, 2007.
166  Hulme, Doherty, Ngara, New and Lister, 2001
167  Huggins, C. 2002
168  IBNET, 2012
169  WASREB, 2011
170  GWP, 2015

2002.[171] The successful implementation of this water sector reform had, however, to be contextualized within the changing political and economic environment in Kenya under the Constitution of Kenya 2010, through amendments brought in the Water Act 2016.[172] But these were not the first reforms in the history of Kenya.

This chapter illustrates key policies, laws and strategies that guide the road to the water sector reforms in Africa by drawing on examples from the Kenyan case. These include the Water Act 2002 and amendments in the Water Act 2016, following the devolution enshrined in the Constitution of Kenya 2010, as well as the Kenya Vision 2030, the Water Master Plan 2030 and the National Environmental Sanitation and Hygiene Policy. These provide a large range of legal frameworks and policies guiding the implementation of water, sanitation and hygiene services by water projects in both rural and urban areas. The analysis will highlight opportunities and constraints related to the financing of the devolved system of governance in the water sector at different levels of policy and management implementation across Africa.

## 4.2 A Roadmap to Integrated Water Resources Management in Kenya

The Government of Kenya (GoK) has undertaken several reforms in the governance of its water sector. Ngigi and Macharia (2007) [173] report that from independence (1963) to 1997, the reforms initiated targeted the improvement of water quality and quantity through adequate financing mechanisms. The 'Water for All by 2000' motto reiterated this aim by initiating a National Water Master Plan (NWMP) in 1974, which led to the establishment of a National Water Development Corporation (NWDC) in 1988 and a new National Water Master Plan in 1999.[174] The first national policy on water resources management and development adopted in Kenya was to address both water resources management (WRM) by the government and water and sanitation servi-ces (WSS) provision by corporate utilities. Its objective was to preserve, conserve and protect available water resources, in order to allocate them in a sustainable way, which should be both economically efficient and financially effective. The Water Act 2002, which was gazetted in October 2002 and came into force in 2003, was an extension of the Integrated Water Resources Management (IWRM) concept contained in the 1999 water policy. It provided an improved legislative framework for more effective management, conservation, use and control of water resources, as well as for the ac-quisition and regulation of rights to use water. It also provided for the regulation and management of water supply and sewerage services.[175]

---

171  Republic of Kenya, 2002
172  Republic of Kenya, 2010a, and Republic of Kenya. 2016a
173  Ngigi and Macharia, 2007
174  Republic of Kenya, 1999
175  Obando, Luwesi, Mathenge, Kinuthia, Wambua, Mutiso and Bader, 2015

After the 2010 constitutional devolution of water and sanitation services, a Water Bill was introduced to parliament in 2012, but it was only enacted recently, in September 2016, for diverse reasons. Nonetheless, the Water Act 2016 was desperately needed not only for the provision of essential water services, but also for the operationalization of the legal and institutional frameworks that guide the administration of the water sector. Its enactment should enable local county governments to achieve the expected outcomes of the 2002 reforms: namely, enhanced accountability, efficiency and affordability; cost recovery, reliability and universal coverage of both water and sanitation services.[176] The WSPs and their boards, as well as the Water Resources Management Authority (WRMA) and supporting catchment management committees and associations, had a key role to play in implementation of this new legislation. They are expected to improve their managerial capacities, abilities and performance to deliver quality services that are affordable to all, while ensuring efficiency and cost recovery in their daily business.[177] Such achievements have to go hand in hand with adequate finance, following the setting-up of a new governance system in the water sector.

## 4.3    Review of the Water Sector Reforms in Kenya

### 4.3.1    Regulatory Frameworks under the Water Act 2002

In 1999, the Kenyan government introduced root-and-branch reforms to overhaul the entire water sector. The Water Act 2002 introduced a far-reaching rationalization of sectoral operations by: (1) bringing the various subsectors under one ministry in charge of water management and development; (2) separating the management of water resources from the provision of water services; (3) de-linking policy-making from day-to-day administration and regulation; (4) devolving some administrative functions to a lower level of the state governance structure; and (5) involving non-government entities in the management of water resources and in the provision of water services.[178] The Water Act 2002 thus introduced new water management institutions to govern water and sanitation services, along with new legal and institutional frameworks and water policies that recognized tacitly the right of each citizen to have access to water and sanitation services (Figure 4.1).

---

176  Luwesi, Kinuthia, Mutiso, Akombo, Doke and Ruhakana, 2015
177  Luwesi and Wambua, 2015
178  Mathenge, Luwesi, Shisanya, Mahiri, Akombo and Mutiso, 2014

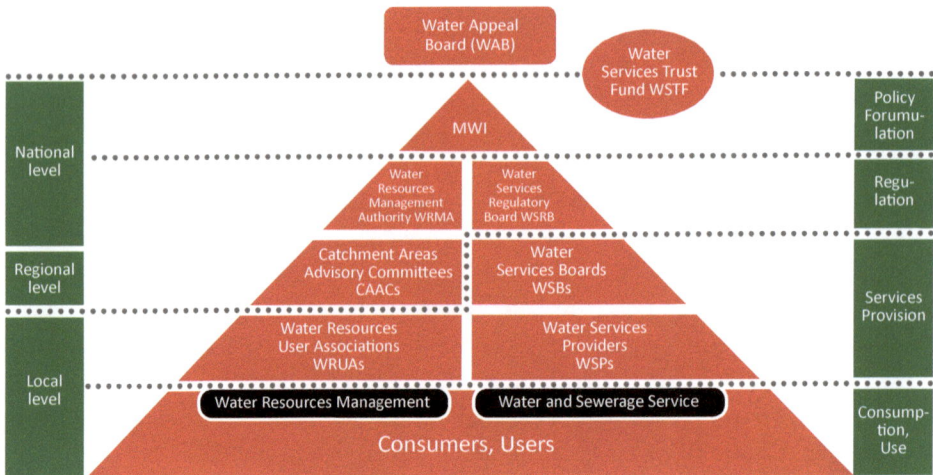

**Figure 4.1.** Legal and institutional set-up of the 2002 water sector reforms in Kenya.

The Ministry of Water and Irrigation (MWI) had the responsibility of overseeing the overall sector, while focusing on sector coordination, monitoring and control; policy formulation, and resource mobilization.[179] The ministry delegated its key functions to autonomous sector institutions, namely water resources management and development to an autonomous public authority and communal associations, and water services provision to autonomous private water companies and corporate suppliers. This devolution of responsibility through separation of policy and regulation from service provision and water resources management has first and foremost improved the mechanisms of accountability and transparency in the water and sanitation services and resources management subsectors.[180]

The Water Resources Management Authority, established under section 7 of the Water Act 2002, was given responsibility for effective management of water resources. While water resources remained vested in the state, the water reforms introduced commercialization of water and sanitation services as part of the decentralization process, as well as the participation of stakeholders in the management of national water resources.[181] Hence, new institutions within the WSS subsector were established. These included the Water Services Regulatory Board (WASREB or WSRB), mandated to set standards and regulations for the subsector; the Water Appeal Board (WAB), designated to adjudicate in disputes; eight water services boards (WSBs) deemed to be responsible for the efficient and economical provision of water services; the Water Services Trust Fund (WSTF), formed to finance pro-poor investments; and water services providers (WSPs), licensed as agents for the provision of water and sewerage services, while utilizing acceptable business principles in their operations.[182]

---

179  MEWNR and JICA, 2013
180  Lonsdale, Wilkins, and Ling, 2011
181  Republic of Kenya, 2002.
182  K'akumu, 2008

## 4.3.2 Implementation of the Water Act 2002

### 4.3.2.1 Organization of the Implementation of the Water Sector Reforms

With the reforms of the whole water sector, the different subsectors underwent a radical transformation. The implementation of these principles triggered a wide-ranging restructuring of these subsectors and led to the creation of new institutions (Table 4.1). The Water Sector Reform Secretariat (WSRS) was formed as a transitional unit in the MWI to oversee the formation of the new water sector institutions. The following subsections focus on the roles played by key intervening actors formed thereafter.

| Institution | Roles and responsibilities |
| --- | --- |
| 1. Ministry of Water and Irrigation (MWI) | • Develop legislation<br>• Formulate policies and strategies<br>• Coordinate sector activities and provide guidance<br>• Monitor and evaluate sector activities<br>• Plan overall sector investment<br>• Mobilize resources |
| 2. Water Services Regulatory Board (WASREB) | • Regulate water services provision<br>• Monitor water services boards and providers<br>• Issue licences to water services boards<br>• Set up standards for water services provision<br>• Develop guidelines (water tariffs, etc) |
| 3. Water Services Boards (WSBs) | • Provide efficient and economical water services<br>• Develop water and sewerage facilities<br>• Plan and implement investment programmes<br>• Rehabilitate and replace infrastructure<br>• Apply regulations on water services and tariffs<br>• Procure and lease water and sewerage facilities<br>• Contract WSPs |
| 4. Water Services Providers (WSPs) | • Provide water and sanitation services<br>• Ensure good customer relations and adequate sensitisation<br>• Maintain assets<br>• Achieve performance levels set by WASREB |
| 5. Water Services Trust Fund (WSTF) | • Finance the provision of water and sanitation to disadvantaged and under-served groups<br>• Fund pro-poor projects to end their water poverty |
| 6. Water Appeal Board (WAB) | • Arbitrate water-related disputes and conflicts between institutions and organizations |
| 7. National Water Conservation and Pipeline Corporation (NWCPC) | • Build dams and drill boreholes |
| 8. Kenya Water Institute (KEWI) | • Conduct training and research on water-related issues |

**Table 4.1.** Institutions created under the Water Act 2002

### 4.3.2.2    Roles of the Water Services Providers

A majority of the rural population of Kenya (58%) and of those living in informal urban settlements continue to use unimproved water sources, while most people in cities and urban areas (62%) have access to safe water and sanitation services. This difference in water and sanitation services accessibility is generally due to the lack of adequate infrastructure in rural areas.[183] Hence, most rural populations rely on water from streams, lakes and ponds for their domestic provision. The 2002 water sector reforms aimed at reducing that disparity between urban and rural areas by establishing private and community led WSPs to develop water sources, improve water quality and supply water and sanitation services to all. This has enabled the government to alleviate the unmet demand of the rapidly growing population in urban areas and subsequently tackle issues arising from the degradation of water catchments and climate change through targeted water development investments. For this strategy to succeed, a regulator of water services was appointed to establish the rules of competition among WSPs.[184]

### 4.3.2.3    Roles of the Water Services Regulatory Board

The Water Services Regulatory Board (WASREB), established under section 46 of the Water Act, is charged with the responsibility of setting standards for equitable water services provision to all, as well as licensing and monitoring WSPs across Kenya for fair competition.[185] The WASREB ensures sustainable provision of water and sanitation services to all by WSPs, using both soft-core tactics and hard-core logistics. The soft components of its interventions encompass good governance (policies, strategies and institutional frameworks), enhanced financial resources and improved technological innovations. Hard components include physical investments, and materials and equipment for operations and maintenance of investments. On the revenue side, WASREB ensures that service providers install more meters on existing connections, even though they seem to be facing stiff resistance to any rise in water tariffs.[186]

To operate a water system in Kenya, a private company or community-based organization must apply to its regional board for a service provision agreement. This agreement details the expectations for service, as well as the tariff structures, which are generally based on the structure set at the national level. More importantly, any changes to the agreed tariff structure must be approved in advance by the regional board, and must be justified. This type of public oversight of utility pricing is positive in principle, but has been hindered in the past in Kenya by the absence of a focused regulator.[187] Since the creation of the WASREB in 2005 and the licensing in 2008 of

---

183  WASREB, 2011
184  WASREB, 2010
185  Luwesi, 2011
186  WASREB, 2014
187  Cook, J 2009

six WSBs – one in each hydrological region – the country has experienced a new way of doing water business.[188] Moreover, in 2008 the WSBs gave permission for 46 WSPs in major cities and rural areas, which has given rise to more competition and donor money flowing into the sector. This has enabled the development of water infrastructure in each region served by WASREB under the control of WSBs. There has also been a transfer of staff and assets from central government to the newly founded WSBs and WSPs, through Legal Notice No. 101 of 12 August 2005, to enable direct public investments in the water services provision subsector.[189]

Other strategic actions adopted by WASREB for financing water infrastructure have included the use of tariffs, fees and fines to cover transaction costs for operations and maintenance (O&M). Naturally, the government Medium Term Expenditure Framework (MTEF) is used to collect taxes from domestic taxpayers and to finance water infrastructure development. However, these traditional sources of financing place many constraints on water development, and thus need to be supplemented by donor and international financial institution (IFI) fund leveraging to enable WSPs to finance additional investments for water infrastructure. This transfer is generally obtained with the backing of WSBs and/or the WSTF.

### 4.3.2.4    *Roles of the Water Services Trust Fund*

The WSTF was established in 2004 under section 83 of the Water Act 2002, to harness financial resources for the water sector, in order to develop water and sanitation within poor communities and areas without adequate water services. The fund has thus far focused on rural areas, rather than on informal settlements in the countryside. Since 2005, WSTF has improved water services in areas that were formerly under-served by means of financial services, giving priority to poor and disadvantaged communities. It has started addressing water and sanitation issues in urban areas with pilot sites that are in peri-urban areas of Nairobi, such as Kibera and Mathare. Between 2007 and 2012, the WSTF received funds from the Government of Kenya and from donor agencies, which it directed to 362 of the poorest locations in the country. These locations were identified in collaboration with the WSBs.[190]

### 4.3.2.5    *Roles of the Water Resources Management Authority*

Section 8(1) of the Water Act 2002 has vested the WRMA with responsibility for developing guidelines for water allocation, as well as for the improvement and development of water resources with community participation. According to the Act, the ownership of 'raw' or in-stream water flow remains with the state in Kenya. In contrast to riparian or first-in-use water rights common in the US, water users are required to pay a

---

188  Daily Nation (December 4), 2008
189  Mumma, 2015
190  MEWNR and JICA, 2013

fee to WRMA, based on the volume extracted.[191] The conservation and development of water and associated natural resources is thus achieved by the national government through WRMA, with the backup of involved local communities gathered within the Water Resources Users' Associations (WRUAs). The latter are considered the true custodians and beneficiaries of these natural resources. Thence, the presence of WRMA as an authority is being progressively felt through the efforts of the WRUAs established in different catchment areas, especially those undergoing higher land degradation in the peri-urban areas and market centres. These areas are highly polluted due to poor management of sewerage and drainage systems.

WRMA, with the support of the National Environment Management Authority (NEMA) has introduced water, sanitation and hygiene (WASH) sensitization meetings to create awareness of proper waste handling, treatment and disposal. They have also conducted regular site visits and public education to curb the effects of uncontrolled quarrying, clay and sand mining, while issuing permits to various water users and mining companies. Other specific strategies include constructing water recycling plants in major towns; promoting standard car wash techniques that save on water and its quality. These include the use of steam jets, the promotion of environmental conservation, waste management, water and sanitation services delivery for disease prevention and control, and public-private partnerships (PPPs) in environmental management. Finally, WRMA efforts have been backed by the Kenya Wildlife Service (KWS), which seeks to mitigate human-wildlife conflict by erecting electric fences along the boundaries of forest reserves and some other protected areas, in order to control the movements of wildlife into the forests and across water bodies.

### 4.3.2.6    Roles of Community Water Management Systems

A number of community-based organizations (CBOs) provide water, sanitation and solid waste management services. But these contributions are, in most cases, neither legally recognized nor encouraged by central and local government.[192] Yet, community involvement in water resources management was the core business of the water sector reforms initiated in Kenya in 1999. To integrate local communities into such participatory water governance, the Water Act 2002 entrusted the WRUAs with the management of all the water resources in their respective catchment areas under the stewardship of the WRMA. WSPs were to deliver commercially viable and affordable water services under the oversight of the WASREB.

Though WRMA and the WRUAs are good for training community members to implement water resources management plans, especially during the design and planning process, other CBOs design and implement these plans wherever there is no formal WRUA or WSP. This approach removes the sole burden of the implementation of the reforms from designated legal bodies to tacit community systems, which combine

---

191  WSP, 2012
192  K'akumu, 2008

both water resources management and relevant water and sanitation services delivery.[193] Since the Water Act 2002 forbids governmental agencies and any other body, CBOs included, to assume simultaneously the roles of both water resources management and water services provision, these self-help groups were urged to be organized either in WRUAs or in WSPs for them to be recognized by the law. Scrapping the traditional mandates of community water management systems (CWMS) to supply water services and manage water resources simultaneously constitutes a major challenge facing the water sector reforms across Africa.[194] Some under-served areas still maintain their water resources and services through the stewardship of either unregistered self-help groups or district water officers (DWOs).[195]

### 4.3.2.7    Roles of the Water Appeal Board (WAB)

The Water Appeal Board (WAB) was established under section 84 of the Water Act 2002. Section 85(2) gives the board the power to adjudicate in disputes within the water sector. According to WRMA (2010),[196] by the end of 2009, illegal water abstractions had been reduced by approximately 30% in the upper parts of most of the catchments, and by 70% in the middle and lower zones. Also, about 21.9% of large-scale water users and 78.1% of small-scale ones were complying with the new regulations. Only seven cases of gross offences were filed with the WAB; a decision was made and the parties complied with the ruling of the WAB.

### 4.3.2.8    Challenges Facing the Implementation of the Water Act 2002

There is still a need for a number of key subsector policies and strategies that would formally recognize the universal right of access to water and sanitation, as envisaged under Sustainable Development Goal number 6 (SDG 6), in order to tackle institutional and operational weaknesses of the water sector from 2002 and beyond.[197] The Ministry of Water and Irrigation[198] recognizes that the current coverage of water services in urban areas is 58%. Besides, the repayment of the servicing loans made to service providers by the National Treasury to develop water and sewerage infrastructure is not up to date, which renders the sector ineligible for more credits and unattractive to money lenders and other financial markets.

The third challenge is the recorded low water use efficiency rates in irrigation. While targets for 2020 and 2030 remain at 80% and 90% for water coverage, the unaccounted-for water (UfW) revenue, which was targeted to fall to 30% in 2015 (as per the National Water Services Strategy 2007-2015), actually increased from 42% to

---

193  Huggins, 2002
194  Mathenge, Luwesi, Shisanya, Mahiri, Akombo and Mutiso, 2014, and Kitissou, 2004
195  Förch, 2009
196  WRMA, 2010
197  IUCN, 2016
198  Republic of Kenya, 2016b

43% in the 2015/16 financial year. Widespread unauthorized and unregulated water abstractions are reported, along with undeterred water pollution. As a remedy, new policies and engineering designs are required to ensure that every drop used is accounted for. Besides, the WRMA should ensure that every abstracted water resource is accounted for within the framework of water use charges and pollution regulation. Finally, the government needs deliberate policies and decisions on how to continuously improve water sector performance and relevant financing mechanisms for the implementation of the newly enacted Water Act 2016, which is a key milestone in meeting the SDG 6 agenda.

### 4.3.3 Amendments Introduced under the Water Act 2016[199]

#### 4.3.3.1 A New Devolved System of Water Governance

In 2010, Kenya adopted a new constitution. Article 43(1) enshrines the human right to water and sanitation for all. Specifically, it states that every person has the right 'to accessible and adequate housing and to reasonable standards of sanitation', as well as the right to 'clean and safe water in adequate quantities'.[200] Under this constitution, the country political governance is devolved in a two-tier system, comprising a national government and 47 county governments. The roles and responsibilities of the national and county governments are defined in the fourth schedule of the constitution. One of the key provisions of the constitution is that water resources, as well as public lands, are to be managed by the national government, with county governments providing water and sanitation services.

In line with that provision, the Kenya Vision 2030 suggests the construction of dams, large pipeline projects and an extension of urban water supplies; the establishment of a water harvesting and storage facility; and the development of water resources information and monitoring systems to improve the provision of water and sanitation services and water resources management. For that reason, the 2010 constitution provides for an 'equalization fund' to enable increased per capita availability of, and access to, safe water and sanitation services, as well as irrigation water, even in marginal and dry lands (Article 204). The constitution gave the mandate to supply water and sanitation to the county governments, in order to enhance and secure the gains achieved by the water sector reforms of 2002. However, a transitional period of three years has been decreed from the last general election of 2013 to full enforcement of these constitutional arrangements. Nonetheless, proposals have been made under the Water Act 2016 to align the existing institutional frameworks to these arrangements. The proposed legislation outlines the mandate and functions of six major institutions, namely the Water Resources Authority (WRA), the National Water Harvesting and Storage Authority (NWHSA), the Water Works Development Agencies (WWDA), the Water

---

199 All information under this sub-section is derived from the Water Act, 2016 (Republic of Kenya, 2016a)
200 Republic of Kenya, 2010a

Services Regulatory Board (WASREB), the Water Tribunal (WT) and the Water Sector Trust Fund (WSTF). (Figure 4.2).

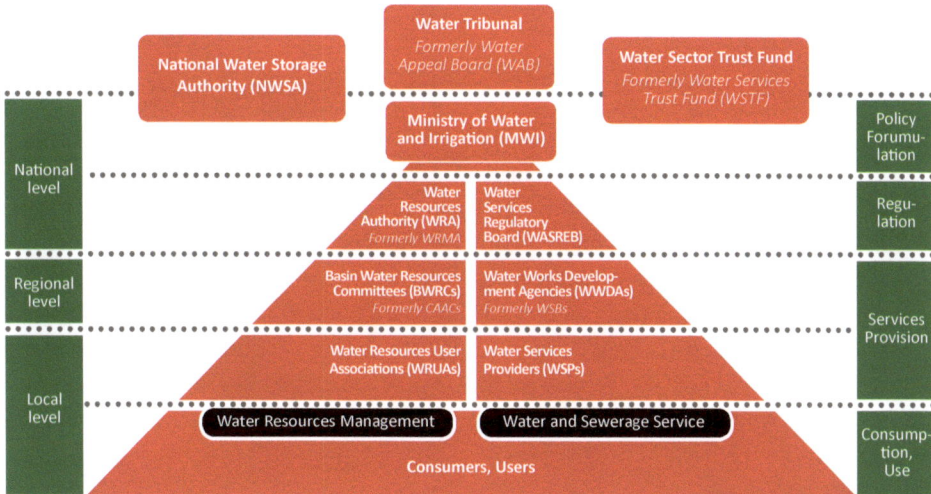

**Figure 4.2.** Amendments of the legal and institutional frameworks under the Kenya Water Act 2016.[201]

### 4.3.3.2    Roles of the Water Resources Authority (WRA)

Under section 11(2) of the Water Act 2016, WRMA has a new corporate name: the Water Resources Authority (WRA). It is a body corporate with perpetual succession and a common seal, capable of suing and being sued. It works at the national level to regulate water resources through basin water resources committees (BWRCs) situated at the basin level. The latter have the mandate vested on the national government to conserve and rehabilitate catchment areas, in order to ensure sustainable in-stream water flow and quality. The authority will advise the Cabinet Secretary on the management and use of water resources and flood control; formulate standards and monitor their implementation; regulate the management and use of water resources, enforce the regulations and the processing of water permits; and collect water permit fees. The act also strengthens the WRA's mandate by giving it a key role in regulating flood management. Besides, several BWRCs and WRUAs have been established to provide a platform for the participation of private investors and businesses in water resources management. These include major water abstractors, such as multipurpose dams, large irrigation schemes and other agricultural water users.

### 4.3.3.3    Roles of the National Water Harvesting and Storage Authority

Under section 32(2) the NWHSA is established to undertake two major functions on behalf of the national government: the development of national public water works

---

201  World Bank, 2016

for water resources storage and flood control; and the maintenance and management of the national public water works infrastructure for water resources storage. The NWHSA will thus be responsible for the work of the water harvesting and storage boards (WHSBs).

### 4.3.3.4    Roles of the Water Works Development Agencies

The new corporate WWDAs are established under section 68 in place of water services boards (WSBs). They will likely serve the same geographical areas under the jurisdiction of the former WSBs to: (i) develop, maintain and manage national public water works and the relevant investment plans; (ii) operate the water works and provide water services as a water services provider, until such a time as responsibility for the operation and management of the water works are handed over to a county government; (iii) provide technical support to the WSPs; and (iv) facilitate the establishment of cross-county WSPs. These service providers may enter into PPP agreements to raise commercial financing upon approval by the WASREB, in agreement with the county governments concerned.

### 4.3.3.5    Roles of the Water Services Regulatory Board

Under section 70(1), the WASREB is principally mandated to protect the interests and rights of consumers in the provision of water services. Its roles are restricted to: (i) developing and prescribing national standards for water provision; (ii) setting and enforcing licence conditions and accrediting water services providers; (iii) evaluating and recommending water and sewerage tariffs to the county WSPs; (iii) advising the government on the nature, extent and conditions of financial support to be accorded to water services providers; (iv) making regulations and maintaining a national database and information system on water services; (vi) making recommendations on how to provide basic water services to marginalized areas; and (vii) monitoring and evaluating compliance with standards, as well as progress in the implementation of the water strategy.

### 4.3.3.6    Roles of the Water Sector Trust Fund

The mandate of the WSTF has been expanded under the Water Act 2016. It is to serve both the water resources management and the water services subsectors. (Which is why its name changed from the Water Services Trust Fund to the Water Sector Trust Fund.) Under section 114, the WSTF will keep conducting its financing operations at the community level and within under-served poor urban areas. It also has a mandate to provide conditional and unconditional grants to the counties, as well as to researchers working in the area of water resources management and water services (sewerage and sanitation included). To raise sufficient funds for its operations, the WSTF will seek partnerships with donors, the private sector and other entities. It will supplement its part of the national and county governments' budgets with the equalization fund, donations, grants and bequests, as well as other funds payable into the fund or under any Act. This funding will mainly depend on the expertise of its personnel and the six licensed Water Services Boards (WSBs) to deliver the expected water and sanitation services. Both WSPs and WSBs will work in consultation with community representatives on matters not directly related to infrastructure development.

It should be noted that the WSTF will mainly assist in financing the development and management of water services within marginalized and under-served areas. It will also get support from community-led initiatives (self-help groups) for the sustainable management of water resources. It will operate on the principle that the development of water services in rural areas and under-served poor urban areas is not commercially viable for service provision by a licensed WSP.

### 4.3.3.7    Roles of the Water Tribunals

Subordinate courts are appointed by the Judicial Service Commission (under section 119) to act as Water Tribunals, in order to hear, determine and arbitrate in cases and appeals at the instance of any person or institution directly affected by the decisions or orders of the Cabinet Secretary, the Water Resources Authority or water basin organizations, the regulatory or storage boards or any other person acting under the authority of the Cabinet Secretary.

## 4.4    Review of Financial Flows to the Water Sector

### 4.4.1    Public Financing Mechanisms under the Water Act 2002

Under the Water Act 2002, there were three main sources of funding for Kenyan water institutions: the national government funds, internally generated funds and donor contributions. Development partners' donations, grants and loans represented almost a third of the total funding of the water sector.[202] A third of these donations and grants were channelled through the government budget, while the remaining two-thirds were disbursed outside the budget. Overall expenditure by the water sector subsequently increased significantly. While more funds were available, there was no discernible indication that more of the GoK funds were being directed to the new water sector institutions. Conversely, donor funds showed a strong tendency towards the new water sector institutions.[203]

Hence, in October 2006, the GoK initiated a Sector-Wide Approach (SWAp) to harmonize the activities of development partners, the coordination and implementation of projects in the wider water sector. The SWAp helped to improve the sector dialogue between the ministry in charge of water and the donors, and to strengthen

---

202  Republic of Kenya, 2010b
203  Republic of Kenya, 2014

cross-sectoral links. A common policy framework for the sector, and common sector programme and strategy as well as joint monitoring and evaluations were developed by the major donor agencies.[204]

The annual water sector review carried out in 2007 revealed, among other things, that the sector interventions were fragmented and needed strong coordination to foster the alignment of donor projects. All the development partners involved in the water sector decided to form a Water Sector Technical Group (WSTG) to harmonize their projects and a Water Sector Working Group (WSWG) to coordinate their work with the government programme. Since 2012, the WSTG has been led by a chair that rotates on an annual basis around the members of a troika, consisting of Germany, the Netherlands and Sweden.[205]

Some community-run small-scale water systems play a critical role in supplying consumers in the peri-urban and rural areas of Kenya. The importance of the role these providers play has been recognized in the recent reforms of the sector in 2016, which provide for a legal and regulatory framework that takes into account the way in which community-based organizations' engage in water services provision outside major towns and cities with support from the WSTF. This will certainly solve some of the challenges that these service providers often experience and which hinder their ability to provide reliable services to consumers and to expand their coverage.[206] Some of the most notable problems are related to their limited management capacity, low operating revenues and lack of access to finance. Public funds to improve these systems are largely absent, since the resources needed are allocated to developing new water sources and systems in very low-income areas with poor access. At the same time, domestic banks do not typically finance investment in water infrastructure because of the long-term risk of infrastructure finance and the perceived lack of creditworthiness of small-scale water providers.[207]

Another key constraint affecting the scaling-up of the programme is the perceived lack of willingness on the part of the WSBs – the agencies that regulate community water projects – to license communities to engage in water services delivery. The WSBs recognize that a lender will not be willing to grant a loan to a project that cannot recover its investment cost or does not have the exclusive legal right to supply water in its service area. This is fundamental, because it is a project's cashflow that generates investment, and its creditworthiness comes from the project's ability to repay debt.[208]

---

204  USAID, 2009
205  Republic of Kenya, 2014
206  Obando, Luwesi, Mathenge, Kinuthia, Wambua, Mutiso and Bader, 2015
207  WASREB, 2014
208  Republic of Kenya, 2016b

### 4.4.2    Financial Provisions under the Water Act 2016 [209]

Section 127 recalls that the financial year covers a period of 12 months, beginning on 1 July. The budget estimates for revenue and expenditure are prepared three months before the commencement of each financial year by each body corporate (Appendix 4.1). Section 128(2) recommends that the annual estimates should make provision for all the estimated expenditure of the respective body corporate for the financial year concerned, and in particular should provide for: (a) the payment of salaries, allowances and other charges in respect of the staff of the body corporate; (b) the payment of pensions, gratuities and other charges and benefits which are payable out of the funds of the body corporate; (c) the maintenance of the buildings and grounds of the body corporate; (d) the funding of training, research and development of activities of the body corporate; and (e) the creation of such funds to meet future or contingent liabilities in respect of benefits, insurance or replacement of buildings or installations, and equipment; and in respect of such other matters as the body corporates may consider necessary.

All income from water permits, abstraction and water user fees should be entirely used for the conservation and management of water resources (section 132). Water resources and storage authorities, services regulator and boards, as well as water works agencies, may retain the revenue from permit charges, water user fees, regulatory levy, licence fees and any other authorized charges and should use such revenue to meet the costs incurred in the performance of their functions (section 130).

The licensed WSPs holding county or national public assets on behalf of the public through water services bills and other sources, should use all funds collected for water services entirely for the purpose of covering costs for the provision of water services and asset development, according to regulations made by the regulator. Under section 131(2), the licensed WSPs are not required to pay any fees for the use of public assets for the provision of water services, other than to repay loans acquired for the development of those assets.

Finally, section 129 (1) charges everybody corporate with keeping proper accounting books and records of account of the income, expenditure, assets and liabilities, to allow the auditor general to conduct his auditing within a period of three months after the end of each financial year. The annual accounts of the body corporate shall be prepared, audited and reported upon in accordance with the provisions of the constitution and the Public Audit Act 2015.

### 4.4.3    Financial Trends in the Water Sector

The Kenya Vision 2030 programme covers the country's flagship water projects, which should help drive the economy and help Kenya become a middle-income country. These include the development and implementation of effective water resources ma-

---

209  All information under this sub-section is exclusively drawn from The Water Act, 2016 (Republic of Kenya. 2016a)

nagement programmes; the construction of water storage structures; the expansion of the total area under irrigation; the rehabilitation and expansion of existing irrigation infrastructure; the rehabilitation and expansion of existing urban water and sewerage schemes; and the development of the rural water supply.[210] Since the mobilization of funds for the water sector is guided by the need to address poverty, illiteracy and disease (health), the Government of Kenya has prioritized and committed itself to the provision of enough water for agriculture, industrial development and domestic use. The expected results include an improvement in people's incomes; a reduction in poverty; and improved health.[211]

Since 1993, when the government brought the various subsectors under the single roof of the then Ministry of Water Development, and the reforms commenced in the water sector, financial flows to the sector have increased more than tenfold: from just under 4 billion Kenyan shilling (KES) in the financial year 2002/03 to KES 37 billion in 2011/12; and from KES 37 billion to KES 62.3 billion in 2016/17 (Figure 4.3 and Figure 4.4).[212] The water sector reforms and government policy of ring-fencing – with high sector revenues, good governance, organizational competence, financial management and budgetary discipline – are among the factors that have contributed to this development, and which have brought positive financial flows to the sector after a decade.[213] The National Water Policy of 1999 and the Water Act of 2002 laid the groundwork for the water sector reforms of the past decade or so. The reforms focused on contributing significantly to an acceleration in the social and economic development of the country. They were mainly guided by international standards, the achievement of which has brought visible improvement to the sector in terms of efficiency, accountability and timeliness in procurement of goods and services.[214]

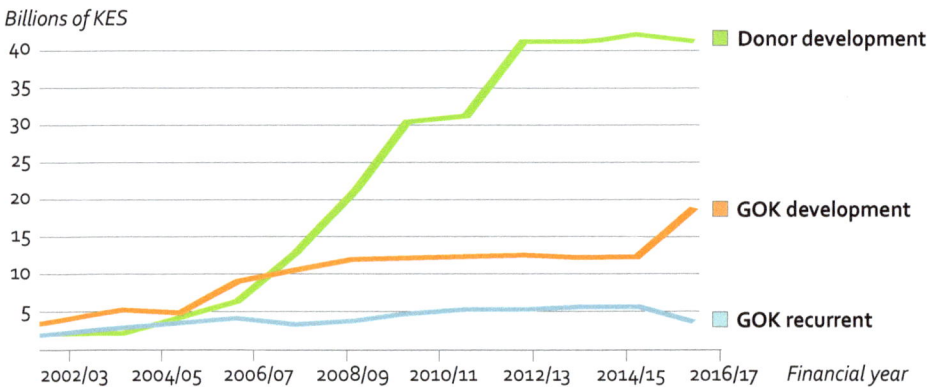

**Figure 4.3.** Financial flows to the water sector in Kenya 2002–17 (billion KES) [215]

---

210 Republic of Kenya, 2007, and TWSB, 2010
211 Republic of Kenya, 2016b
212 Kinuthia, and Lakin, 2016
213 Republic of Kenya, 2016c
214 The Republic of Kenya, 2016d
215 Adapted from Republic of Kenya, 2010b, 2012 and 2016

Millions of KES

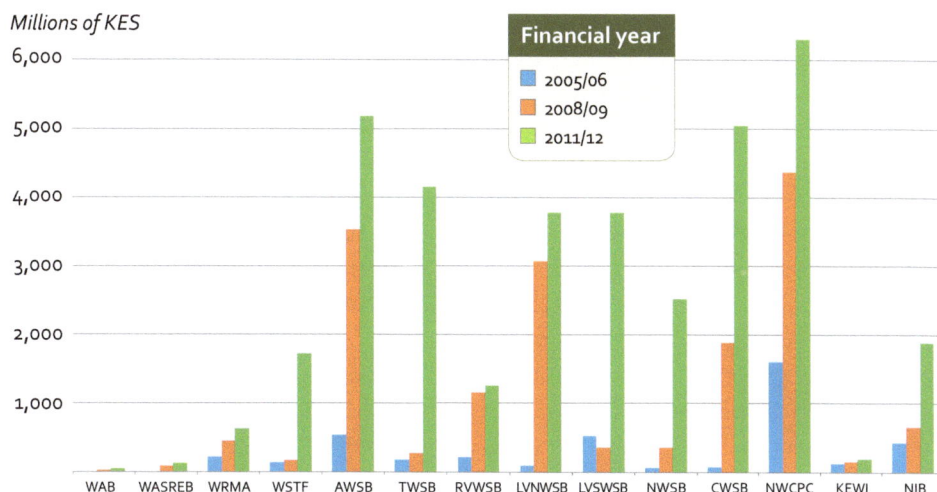

| Water body corporate / authority | |
|---|---|
| WAB: Water Appeal Board | LVNWSB: Lake Victoria North Water Services Board |
| WASREB: Water Services Regulatory Board | LVSWSB: Lake Victoria South Water Services Board |
| WRMA: Water Resources Management Authority | NWSB: Northern Water Services Board |
| WSTF: Water Services Trust Fund | CWSB: Coast Water Services Board |
| AWSB: Athi Water Services Board | NWCPC: National Water Conservation and Pipeline Corporation |
| TWSB: Tana Water Services Board | KEWI: Kenya Water Institute |
| RVWSB: Rift-Valley Water Services Board | NIB: National Irrigation Board |

**Figure 4.4.** Funds made available to water body corporates and authorities in Kenya 2002–2012.[216]

## 4.4.4    *Challenges and Constraints for Financing the Water Sector in Kenya*

There are many constraints affecting finance in the water sector. First, the constitution enacted in 2010 has come with many innovations that accompany a devolved system of governance. This is creating some challenges to the water sector, as it is not bound to administrative boundaries but is compelled to take the direction needed for the full implementation of the constitution.[217] For investors to continue to find the sector competitive, water sector policies must clearly show how it will realign its programme with the new constitutional requirements, while safeguarding the gains realized over the last decade or so of reform. Other constraints include the negative influence of the following factors:[218] (i) slow absorption of funds by projects; (ii) failure of services providers (consultants, contractors, suppliers) to strictly adhere to the programme of works; (iii) slow disbursement of funds by both donors and the ministry, due to internal bureaucratic processes; (iv) failure to be timely in progress reporting; (v) staff and assets transfer plan; (vi) inadequate budgeting skills by institutions, as indicated

---

216  Adapted after Republic of Kenya, 2006, 2009 and 2012.
217  Luwesi and Wambua, 2015
218  Luwesi and Wambua, 2015

by underestimation of project expenditure; (vii) lack of efficient coordination among the numerous financiers in the sector; and (viii) weak organizational and budgetary discipline among sector institutions.

Other financing challenges include the lack of collateral for securing loans; the high costs of title deeds (for land legalization and regularization); external delivery costs; and the shortage of capital for investment. Even when credit institutions do agree to finance infrastructure projects for poor neighbourhoods, they often stumble in the process. The right conditions for financing just do not exist in these areas. For example, loans for infrastructure may sometimes have been made to associations that do not have legal existence and no equity, including some CBOs, WRUAs and CWMSs in the early stage of the implementation of the 2002 reforms. Besides, the process of land legalization and re-zoning, an almost universal requirement for the provision of urban water and sanitation, has given rise to additional – often very burdensome – costs.[219]

These requirements often make the cost of infrastructure unaffordable to low-income households. They have neither the money to invest in infrastructure nor the support of others who could lend to them, and so they turn to the government for financing. National governments can and do borrow both externally and internally; but they prefer to borrow for projects that are likely to pay off the loans (such as ports, roads or power plants) rather than for those with slow cashflows, like water services. Moreover, poor households living in rural areas do not always appreciate the net benefits of a title deed or a zoning variance, since most of them live on ancestral lands.[220] External delivery costs include the cost of the off-site main piping system that brings water to a neighbourhood and drains wastewater away; and the cost of a sewage treatment plant. These costs are increasingly becoming a requirement for any new water and sanitation system, but are often overlooked in economic analyses. [221]

Other barriers to financial flows into the water sector include: (i) weaknesses in the management and governance systems of decentralized units; (ii) affordability constraints due to difficulty in covering the cost of increasing tariffs in WSS; (iii) short repayment time of any financing that is available; (iv) undercapitalized balance sheets of WSS systems and corporates, leading to high debt levels and low equity; (v) lack of bankable projects due to poor project preparation capacity; and (vi) high risk profile and difficulties in managing risks.[222]

To overcome these constraints and challenges, and to keep attracting investors, there is a need to put in place measures that would ensure the timely release of funds. The harmonization of fund disbursement by development partners would also ensure timeliness in the release of funds. Full harmonization of procurement procedures by development partners and the GoK would ensure efficiency. A complete transfer of assets and staff to the sector institutions and a guarantee that staff salaries are paid from

219  Solo, Eduardo and Joyce, 1993
220  Ehlers, 2014
221  Solo, Eduardo and Joyce, 1993, and Daily Nation (October 8), 2015
222  Luwesi and Wambua, 2015

the budget of these institutions are recommended.[223] There is another requirement for the effective channelling of funds to the sector. This will require sensitization and capacity building of the individual staff on public expenditure efficient allocation and the budgeting process implementation. Furthermore, there is a need to strengthen budget monitoring of all activities related to projects and programmes.[224]

Finally, financial data collection from projects and programmes should also be strengthened. The sector should fast-track the development of the Water Sector Investment Programme (SIP), which will help to attract investment in the sector, including by NGOs, civil society organizations and the private sector. In this regard, donors providing funding to NGOs need to inform the ministry. And the sector should develop a mechanism for ensuring that NGOs in the water sector document annually their spending and their results, and account for these to the sector and the public.[225]

## 4.5    New Market Opportunities for Water Finance

Traditional sources of financing for the water sector impose many constraints on its development. There is a need for innovative thinking and risk-taking from both the public and private actors operating in the water sector. The government should provide both a stable macroeconomic framework and good regulation of the water sector, in order to ensure political and public confidence, and incentives to attract private investments. There are many prospects for improving finance in the water sector using public-private partnerships, whether in the form of microfinance, banking loans, lease or concession schemes.[226] These innovative financing mechanisms have the potential to enhance the creditworthiness of WSPs and WRUAs to allow them to have access to funds other than the 3Ts (tariffs, taxes and transfers). However, they may be hampered if there is a lack of understanding among lenders and investors, as well as a lack of funds at the decentralized level for small utilities, which are unable to access market-based payable finance. These issues must first be addressed to enable PPPs to take off smoothly in the water sector (Box 4.1).

The Water Act 2002 creates a revolving fund, which consists of grant money to finance the public cost of the preparation and structuring of complex projects, including private sector participation and other innovative structures. This fund is generally used in the preparation and structuring of project bids (including legal, financial and technical advisory costs) at both the tendering and the negotiation phases. The fund shall rely on the best practices and model clauses enshrined in the legal agreements for PPPs in the water sector, in order to attract more and alternative funding sources.

There is also a need for a change in thinking and attitudes toward potential investors. Funding sources can be provided by local or expatriate individual lenders or

---

223  Förch, Winnegge and Thiemann, 2010
224  Förch, Winnegge and Thiemann, 2010
225  IBNET, 2012
226  Winpenny, 2003

shareholders, as well as by private or public institutions. Therefore, WSPs and WRUAs need to be organized into pools of borrowers, so that the risks from bulk loans are shared and so that experience is transferred from large-scale to smaller borrowers.

With considerable public financial resources available in the water sector, the size of the market for a loan-linked product is likely to be limited in the medium term. However, public funds are not adequate to build the infrastructure required to effectively meet the demand for water services; hence the increased focus on cost-recovery tariffs and the important initiatives in hand to access supplementary financial resources from the private sector.

It is therefore important for the Government of Kenya to upgrade its governance structures at the lowest level of catchment management, in order to enhance capacity in identifying and preparing projects that are suited to the demands of commercial lenders. This will make financial innovations flexible to all sorts of borrowers. The use of partnerships and aggregation in utilities may also enable knowledge and skill transfer, and improve the credit history of WSPs and WRUAs. The latter should enhance their creditworthiness and capacity to take commensurate risks by, among other things, introducing a culture of record keeping in accounting and finance.

Donors should be obliged to meet their commitments to increase aid to the water sector. Overall overseas development assistance (ODA) for water should be doubled, as a first step, and the share of water in total ODA should increase substantially from its current level. Individual donors are urged to contribute their share to this target, depending on the size of their current aid to the water sector, to promote innovativeness in water finance.

## 4.6    Public–Private Partnerships and Concession Agreements

Commercial banks and other financial institutions play an important role in financing both public and private sector service providers. The private water sector may contribute significantly to investments flowing in water supply, sanitation and irrigation. The public sector shall thus invest in environmental protection to ensure that responsive regulations, legislation and institutions are in place to provide specific incentives to private investors.

The growing involvement of the large and/or international private sector in water supply and sanitation sub-sector is justified by four main reasons:[227] (1) *Financial*: government passes on the cost and work of raising funds; (2) *Political*: there is a growing number of reforms being conducted in the water sector to enable private companies to operate freely (e.g. raising tariffs, collecting unpaid bills, reducing the workforce); (3) *Expertise*: large and international private companies bring essential know-how in some technical and economic fields; and (4) *Risk-sharing*: private companies are typically better at handling risks.

---

227 GWP, 2005

Government departments (public authority) enter into partnership with private entities (developer) to design, construct, finance, operate and maintain an asset that will be used by or is otherwise valuable to the public. New methods of contracting, procurement and enforcement for constructions (e.g. design-build), require a single private entity (generally a consortium) to be responsible for all the project functions, including design, construction, financing, operation and maintenance, as outlined under a 'concession agreement'. This has enabled government agencies to procure new waterways and wastewater treatment facilities, or large hydropower plants and irrigation schemes in record time and cost-effectively, and far more higher-quality projects with reduced risks. In exchange, the developer receives 'toll revenues' (on which the developer takes both demand risk and toll collection revenue risk) or 'availability payments' (on which the developer takes financial risk associated with performing the work according to agreed performance metrics).[228]

An example of such innovative partnerships is South Africa's Touwsrivier Solar Project bond.[229] This bond of 1 billion South African Rand was launched to finance the construction of a 44 MWp (megawatt peak) concentrated photovoltaic plant in an economically impoverished part of the country ('green bond') with a 15-year maturity and 11% coupon. One of its innovative features is its amortizing repayment structure, which is similar to that of a mortgage. Another feature of this project are the incentives provided by the government through South Africa's Renewable Energy Feed-in Tariff (REFIT) programme. This allows national electric utilities to purchase power from renewable sources at predetermined prices with the backing of the South African Department of Energy. Nonetheless, the main types of PPPs (private involvement or privatization) practised in the water sector during the last decade encompass five major types: contracting out, leasing, concessions, joint ventures and divestiture.[230]

CONTRACTING OUT is a form of partial privatization in which a water undertaking sub-contracts certain functions to private firms (e.g. meter reading; billing; payment through mobile platforms, etc.).

LEASING is a form of private sector involvement that is very common in French-speaking areas and involves a water system being leased to private operators, while remaining in the public domain.

CONCESSIONS are PPPs in which the use of a public water system is conceded to private operators for a new investment or development over a certain period of time (generally 20–25 years), while assets remain in public ownership. For new facilities, concession contracts may take several other forms, including BOOT (Build, Own, Operate, Transfer), BOT (Build, Operate, Transfer), BOL (Build, Operate, and Lease) and BOS (Build, Operate and Sell).

JOINT VENTURES involve operating companies in a solitary business enterprise solely to make profit without actual partnership or incorporation. This form of PPP is also called a 'joint adventure'.

---

228 FHWA, 2015
229 OECD, 2015
230 GWP, 2005

DIVESTITURE: an extreme form of privatization, initiated in England and Wales, in which the full ownership of assets is transferred to private shareholders under stringent public regulations.

It should be noted that micro-finance and community banks also allow poor people to get involved in the financing of small-scale water infrastructure, for both domestic and agricultural use. In all cases, small-scale or community-level private sector involvement is dependent on government economic policies, which can ease access to finance or make it difficult for the poor. The government has a key role in providing a clear regulatory framework, and ensuring that the poor are served and users are protected from excessive costs.

# References

Cook, J. 2009. Microfinance in the Water Supply and Sanitation Sector in Kenya, Washington, DC: University of Washington, Evans School of Public Affairs.

Daily Nation (December 4). 2008. Rising unga and power costs are not enough, wait for your next water bill. Nairobi: Nation Media Group Ltd.

Daily Nation (October 8). 2015. Here's why you should check your land records often. Nairobi: The Nation Media Group.

Ehlers, T. 2014. Understanding the challenges for infrastructure finance. BIS Working Papers No 454. Basel: Bank for International Settlements (BIS), Monetary and Economic Department. Available at:http//:www.bis.org/publ/work454.pdf (Accessed on 12.10.2015).

Förch, G., Winnegge, R. and Thiemann, S. (Eds). 2010. DAAD Alumni Summer School: Financial instruments for integrated watershed management .Final Report. CICD Series No 9. Siegen: Universität Siegen.

Förch, N. 2009. Integrated Water Resources Management for Conflict Transformation– A Study of the Kenyan Water Sector Reforms. Master's Thesis. Berlin: Freie Universität Berlin, Otto-Subr Institut.

GWP. [Global Water Partnership]. 2005. IWRM Toolbox.

GWP. [Global Water Partnership]. 2015. Integrated Water Resources Management in Eastern Africa: Coping with 'Complex Hydrology'. In Technical Focus Papers (TFP) No 7. Stockholm: Elanders.

Huggins, C. 2002. Water policy and law in a water-scarce country. In: Murray-Rust and Blank (eds), The Changing Face of Irrigation in Kenya. Colombo: International Water Management Institute (IWMI).

Hulme M., Doherty, R., Ngara, T., New, M. and Lister, D. 2001. African Climate Change: 1900 – 2100. Climate Research, 17, 145–168.

IBNET. [International Benchmarking Network]. 2012. International Benchmarking for Water and Sanitation Utilities. Available at: www.ibnet.org (Accessed on 17.03.2013).

IUCN. [International Union for Conservation of Nature]. 2016. Knowledge for SDG Action in West Asia and North Africa: R-KNOW Water Governance Best Practices within the Water, Energy,Food and Climate Change Nexus. Amman: IUCN- Regional Office for West Asia. Available at: www.iucn.org/westasia (Accessed on 06.03.2017).

K'akumu, O.A. 2008. Mainstreaming the participatory approach in water resource governance: The 2002 water law in Kenya. Development 51: 56-62.

Kinuthia, J. and Lakin, J. 2016. Kenya: Analysis of the 2016/17 National Budget Estimates. Washingtong, D.C.: International Budget Partnership (IBP). Available at: http://www.internationalbudget.org/wp-content/uploads/ibp-kenya-analysis-of-2016-17-national-budget-estimates-6-2016.pdf (Accessed on 06.03.2016)

Kitissou, M. 2004. Hydropolitics and Geopolitics: Transforming Conflict and Reshaping Cooperation in Africa, Africa Notes, Issue of November-December 2004.

Kundzewicz, Z. W., Mata, L. J., Arnell, N. W., Doll, P., Kabat, P., Jimenez, B., … Shiklomanov, I. A. 2007. Freshwater resources and their management. In M. L. Parry et al. (Eds.), Climate Change 2007: Impacts, Adaptation and Vulnerability. Cambridge: Cambridge University Press.

Lonsdale, J., Wilkins, P. And Ling, T. 2011. Performance Auditing: Contributing to Accountability in Democratic Government. Cheltenham: Edward Elgar Publishing Ltd.

Luwesi, C.N. (Ed.). 2011. Innovative Ways in Financing the Water Sector. Final SWAP/bfz Workshop Report. Mombasa: Bfz and WaterCap, 7-11 November 2011. Available at: http://watercap.org/ (Accessed on 17.03.2013)

Luwesi, C.N. and Wambua, P.P. 2015. Baseline Report: Murang'a County Water Services Management Rationalization and Masterplan. Consultancy Report by the Finance and Human Resource Team. Nairobi: APEC Consulting and BE_Associates.

Luwesi, C.N. and Wambua, P.P. 2015. Baseline Report: Murang'a County Water Services Management Rationalization and Masterplan. Consultancy Report by the Finance and Human Resource Team. Nairobi: APEC Consulting and BE_Associates.

Luwesi, C.N., Kinuthia, W., Mutiso,M.N., Akombo, R.A., Doke, D.A. and Ruhakana, A. 2015. Climate Change, Pro-Poor Schemes and Water Inequality: Strengths and Weaknesses of Kauti Irrigation Water Users' Association, Kenya. In: A. Beyene (Ed.), Agricultural Water Institutions in East Africa. Nordiska Afrikainstitutet, Uppsalla, Current African Issues 63, pp. 43–60.

Mathenge, J.M., Luwesi, C.N., Shisanya, C.A., Mahiri, I., Akombo, R.A., Mutiso, M.N. 2014. Water Security Where Governmental Policies Conflict with Local Practices: The Roles of Community Water Management Systems in Ngaciuma-Kinyaritha, Kenya. International Journal of Innovative Research and Development (IJIRD), Vol. 3 (5), pp. 793-804.

MEWNR. [Ministry of Environment, Water and Natural Resources] and JICA. [Japan International Cooperation Agency]. 2013. The National Water Master Plan 2030 (Final Draft). Nairobi: Nippon Koei Co., Ltd.

Mumma, A. 2015. Kenya's new water law: an analysis of the implications for the rural poor. Paper presented during the Water security 2015 Conference, Parallel 4: Political accountability and water security risks. Oxford: Oxford University, Oxford Martin School, 9 December 2015.

Ngigi, A. and Macharia, D. 2007. Kenya Water Sector Overview. Nairobi: IT Power East Africa.

Obando, J.A., Luwesi, C.N., Mathenge, J.M., Kinuthia, W., Wambua, P.P., Mutiso, M.N., and Bader, E.O. 2015. Performance assessment and evaluation of community participation in water sector governance - The case of Ngaciuma-Kinyaritha catchment, Mount Kenya region. In: A. Beyene (Ed.), Agricultural Water Institutions in East Africa. Nordiska Afrikainstitutet, Uppsala, Current African Issues 63, pp. 23 –42.

OECD. [Organisation for Economic Cooperation and Development]. 2015. Infrastructure Financing Instruments and Incentives. Available at: http://www.oecd.org/finance/private-pensions/Infrastructure-Financing-Instruments-and-Incentives.pdf (Accessed on 06.03.2017)

Republic of Kenya. 1999. National Policy on Water Resource Management and Development. Nairobi: Government Printer.

Republic of Kenya. 2002. The Water Act, 2002. Kenya Gazette Supplement No. 107 (Acts No. 9). Nairobi: Government Printer, pp 287–413.

Republic of Kenya. 2002. The Water Act, 2002. Kenya Gazette Supplement No. 107 (Acts No. 9). Nairobi: Government Printer, pp 287–413.

Republic of Kenya. 2006 Annual National Government Budget Implementation-Review Report Half Year -FY 2005/06. Nairobi: Office of the Controller of Budget.

Republic of Kenya. 2007. Kenya Vision 2030. Available at: http://www.fao.org/fileadmin/user_upload/drought/docs/Vision%202030-%20Popular%20Version.pdf (Accessed on 13.05.2008)

Republic of Kenya. 2009 Annual National Government Budget Implementation-Review Report Half Year -FY 2008/09. Nairobi: Office of the Controller of Budget.

Republic of Kenya. 2010a. The Constitution of Kenya, 2010. Kenya Law Reports, Laws of Kenya. Nairobi: National Council for Law Reporting.

Republic of Kenya. 2010b. Water Sector Strategic Plan (WSSP) 2010-2015. Ministry of Water and Irrigation, Nairobi: Government Printer.

Republic of Kenya. 2012. Annual National Government Budget Implementation-Review Report Half Year -FY 2015/16. Nairobi: Office of the Controller of Budget.

Republic of Kenya. 2014. Strategic Investment Plan. Nairobi: Government Printer.

Republic of Kenya. 2014. Strategic Investment Plan. Nairobi: Government Printer.

Republic of Kenya. 2016a. The Water Act 2016, Kenya Gazette Supplement Acts, Special Issue, Supplement No. 164 (Acts No.43). Nairobi: Government Printer, pp. 1019-1124.

Republic of Kenya. 2016b. Remarks by the cabinet secretary, ministry of water and irrigation Hon. Eugene Wamalwa, during the official opening of the ministerial performance review retreat at wWaterbuck Hotel, Nakuru on13th October 2016. Available at: http://www.water.go.ke/wp-content/uploads/2016/10/CS-Speech-During-Retreat-for-Performance-.pdf (Accessed on 06.03.2017).

Republic of Kenya. 2016b. Remarks by the cabinet secretary, ministry of water and irrigation Hon. Eugene Wamalwa, during the official opening of the ministerial performance review retreat at Waterbuck Hotel, Nakuru on13th October 2016. Available at: http://www.water.go.ke/wp-content/uploads/2016/10/CS-Speech-During-Retreat-for-Performance-.pdf (Accessed on 06.03.2017).

Republic of Kenya. 2016c. Prosperity Amidst Volatility. Budget Watch for 2016/17 (Edition No. 9). Nairobi: Parliamentary Service Commission, Parliamentary Budget Office.

Republic of Kenya. 2016d. Annual National Government Budget Implementation-Review Report Half Year -FY 2015/16. Nairobi: Office of the Controller of Budget.

Solo, T,M., Eduardo, E.P. and Joyce, S. 1993. Constraints in providing water and sanitation services to the urban poor Office of Health. WASH Technical Report No. 85. Washington, D.C.: U.S. Agency for International Development (USAID), Bureau for Research and Development, WASH Task No. 338.

TWSB. [Tana Water Service Board]. 2010. Detailed Design and Supervision for Murang'a North and Murang'a South Bulk Water Supply Project - Design Report Part 1: Feasibility Review. Document No. 10330-FR-C-001/1. Nyeri: Tana Water Services Board (TWSB) & Consultants (Howard Humphreys East Africa Ltd Consulting Engineers).

USAID. [United States Agency for International Development]. 2009. Kenya Water and Sanitation Profile. Available at: http://pdf.usaid.gov/pdf_docs/Pnado931.pdf (Accessed on 12.11.2011).

FHWA. [Federal Highway Authority]. 2015. Availability payment concessions public-private partnerships model contract guide. Available at: http://www.fhwa.dot.gov/ipd/p3/resources/ p3_ core_toll_concession_contract_guide.aspx (Accessed on 08.08.2016).

WSP. [Water and Sanitation Program]. 2012. Sustainable Services for Domestic Private Sector Participation Using Credit Ratings to Improve Water Utility Access to Market Finance in Sub-Saharan Africa. Washington: Water and Sanitation Program Briefing, February 2012.

WASREB. [Water Services Regulatory Board]. 2010. Impact: A Performance Report of Kenya's Water Services Sub-Sector, Issue No 3. Nairobi: RealONE Concept Ltd.

WASREB. [Water Services Regulatory Board]. 2011. Financing Urban Water Services In: Kenya Utility Shadow Credit Ratings. Nairobi: Water and Sanitation Program (WSP).

WASREB. [Water Services Regulatory Board]. 2011. Financing Urban Water Services In: Kenya Utility Shadow Credit Ratings. Nairobi: Water and Sanitation Program (WSP).

WASREB. [Water Services Regulatory Board]. 2014. Assessing options to achieve commercial viability and financial sustainability of water supply and sanitation services. Nairobi: German Cooperation (GiZ).

Winpenny, J. 2003. Financing water for all: Report of the world panel on financing water infrastructure. Marseille: World Water Council (WWC), 3rd World Water Forum (3WWF) and Global Water Partnerships (GWP). Available at: http://www.worldwatercouncil.org/fileadmin/world_water_council/documents_old/Library/Publications_and_reports/CamdessusSummary.pdf (Accessed on 07.05.2008).

World Bank. 2016. Understanding the Kenya 2016 Water Act. Available at: http://2030wrg.org/wp-content/uploads/2016/12/Understanding-the-Kenyan-Water-Act-2016.pdf (Accessed on 06.03.2017).

WRMA. [Water Resources Management Authority]. 2010. Enforcement of Water Use Charges and Water Quality Thresholds in Kenya. WRMA Evaluation Workshop. Meru: Three Steers Hotel, 24-28 January 2010.

# Appendix 4.1: Schedule for Budget Preparation in Kenya

| Activity | Deadline | | Institution responsible |
| --- | --- | --- | --- |
| | National Government | County Government | |
| 1. Issue budget guidelines: to include updated sector composition, budget calendar and key milestones and preliminary resource allocation | End July | End July | National treasury (BSD) / county treasury |
| 2. Strategic planning | End August | End August | Institution responsible for planning |
| Progress report on implementation of Vision 2030 MTP (2008-12) | Mid August | Mid August | Ministry of Planning |
| Expenditure review | End August | End August | Line ministries |
| Update of strategic plans based on new mandate | | | |
| Preparation of annual plans | | | |
| 3. Formulation of macro-fiscal framework | End October | End October | National treasury (MWG, CRA, BEC, BEF)/county treasury |
| Draft BROP | Mid August | Mid August | MWG |
| Update macro-fiscal framework | | | |
| Estimation of resource envelope (indicative) | | | |
| Determination of policy priorities | | | |
| Consultations with CRA | | | |
| Resource allocation to national and county governments, sectors, judiciary and parliament | | | |
| Stakeholder consultation | End August | End August | National/county treasury |
| Update BROP based on stakeholder comments | Mid September | Mid September | MWG |
| Circulate to BEC and BEF members | Mid September | Mid September | National/county treasury |
| BEC/BEF meeting | End September | End September | National/county treasury |
| Submission to national/county executive | Mid October | Mid October | Cabinet/county secretary for finance |
| Approval by national/county executive | End October | End October | |

| Activity | Deadline | | Institution responsible |
| --- | --- | --- | --- |
| | National Government | County Government | |
| 4. Development of budget proposals | Mid December | Mid December | SWG |
| Launch of sector working group | Mid August | Mid August | National/county treasury |
| Preparation of MTEF budget proposals | Mid October | Mid October | Line ministries |
| Public participation | End October | End October | SWG |
| Draft sector reports | Mid November | Mid November | SWG |
| Submit to treasury | Mid December | Mid December | SWG Chairman |
| Review of proposals | Mid December | Mid December | National/county treasury |
| 5. Development and approval of BPS/CFSP, Division of Revenue Bill (DORB) and County Allocation of Revenue Bill (CARB) | Mid February | Mid February | National treasury (MWG, CRA, BEC, BEF)/county treasury |
| Recommendations on division and allocation of revenue based on audited revenue | Mid January | Mid January | CRA |
| Draft BPS/DORB/CARB | Mid January | Mid January | MWG |
| Updating macro-fiscal framework | | | |
| Sharing of resources | | | |
| Circulate draft BPS to BEC and BEF | Mid January | Mid January | National treasury |
| BEC/BEF meeting | End January | End January | National/county treasury |
| Update BPS to incorporate council comments | End January | End January | MWG |
| Develop DORB and CARB | End January | End January | National treasury |
| Submission of BPS to Parliament and CFSP to county assembly for approval | End January | End January | National/county treasury |
| Approval by Parliament/county assembly | Mid February | Mid February | Parliament/county assembly |

| Activity | Deadline | | Institution responsible |
| --- | --- | --- | --- |
| | National Government | County Government | |
| 6. Preparation and approval of programme budgets | End June | End June | Line ministries, national and county treasury / assembly |
| Issue guidelines | Mid February | Mid February | National / county treasury |
| Submission to treasuries (and to national assembly for judiciary and parliament budgets) | Mid March | Mid March | Line ministries / county departments |
| Consolidation | Mid April | Mid April | National/county treasury |
| Submission of budget estimates to national assembly and county assembly for approval | 24 April | 24 April | Cabinet/county cabinet secretary for finance |
| Submit views on the budgets for judiciary and parliament to national assembly | Mid May | Mid May | National Treasury |
| Public hearing | Mid May | Mid May | Relevant committee of Parliament |
| Review by relevant committee of Parliament | End May | End May | Relevant committee of Parliament |
| Committee of Supply | End June | End June | Relevant committee of Parliament |
| Consolidation of national government budget | End June | End June | National treasury |
| Appropriation bill and finance bill passed OR | End June | End June | National/county assembly |
| Vote on account | End June | End June | National/county assembly |
| 7. Budget implementation | Continuous | Continuous | COB, national treasury and county treasury |
| Submission of reports on budget implementation to COB | 15th day of each quarter | 15th day of each quarter | Line ministries |
| Submission of reports on budget implementation to national/county assembly | 45th day of each quarter | 45th day of each quarter | COB |
| Submit supplementary budget for approval by national/county assembly | February | February | National / county treasury |
| 8. Accounting and audit | March | March | National/county treasury, auditor general |
| Submit final accounts to treasury and auditor general | September | September | Line ministries |
| Submit consolidated annual accounts to auditor general | October | October | National/county treasury |
| Submit audited accounts to national/county assembly | December | December | Auditor general |
| Review audit reports by national/county assembly | March | March | National/county assembly |

# 5. Societal Marketing and Resource Mobilisation: Communication and Engagement Methods

Rain gauge measuring instrument in Itare, Western Kenya. Photo credit Sande Murunga, CIFOR.

Most rural communities and water users still believe that they have been abandoned by public governance and national development.

# Summary

- THE SLOW PACE of compliance with water use charges and water quality require-ments is disturbing the overall implementation of the water sector reforms in Sub-Saharan Africa, owing to the reluctance and unwillingness on the part of water users to pay.
- MANAGERS SHOULD ALWAYS create or re-create awareness of the reforms and obtain key stakeholders' agreement on a fair price that tackles consumers' buying power, full cost recovery and the unpredictable watershed environ-mental trends.
- SOCIETAL MARKETING MANAGEMENT provides a framework (SWOT analysis) for reflection and communication for consumer behaviour change through adop-tion of a specific marketing mix or strategy for uptake ('4Ps') that translate the management 'weaknesses' and 'threats' into resources (strengths and opportu-nities), to minimize serious challenges to the management.
- THE MARKETING MIX should take into account the inner beliefs or values of the target group, their perceptions and choice behaviours, expectations and fears to design a very special brand and message that will condition the mind of members of each targeted group and stimulate positive thinking and quick response.
- IF PEOPLE ARE CONSTANTLY reminded to change their behaviour, they are likely to develop favourable attitudes toward the water sector reforms. This may re-inforce their determination to abide by the rules, so that they may enjoy imme-diate and future benefits accruing from the reforms.
- WATERSHED MANAGERS and water service providers need to cluster their stake-holders within different watershed segments, which are groups of needs, to be able to target a leading support group for public relations, promotional activi-ties and publicity.
- THEREFORE, the management needs to carefully plan 'what' and 'how' it tells the public about its performance, using specific messaging tactics.
- ALL THESE ACTIVITIES should reinforce the public conviction that it made the right choice and that the benefits far outstrip the sacrifices.

Chapter 5:

# Societal Marketing and Resource Mobilisation: Communication and Engagement Methods

*Cush Ngonzo Luwesi, Aseye Afi Nutsukpui, Philip Wambua Peter and Amos Yesutanbul Nkpeebo*

## 5.1 Introduction

Legal and institutional frameworks for water supply and watershed management are consistently being reviewed to promote a fair price, in order to tackle the unpredictable environmental trends in water-stressed areas around the globe.[231] Societal marketing management is the backbone of sustainable implementation of these reforms, which aim to communicate and enforce the 'user-pays' and the 'polluter-pays' principles. These are further supported by novel green approaches, such as payment for watershed services (PWS), green water credits (GWC), clean development mechanisms (CDM) and reducing emissions from deforestation and degraded land (REDD+).[232] These schemes have recently been developed on the principle that there are cause and effect relationships between community land use and functioning ecosystems and their services in a landscape.[233] The success of such innovative schemes largely depends on the willingness of local stakeholders to pay and to accept compensation. Anybody or any group that is concerned with, or is interested in, a particular issue concerning the scheme, whether individual members of the community, private companies and civil society organizations, governmental bodies or development partners, is a stakeholder in the scheme.[234] Therefore, a well-defined and voluntary transaction is needed to secure payment for, and the sustainability of, water services – if, and only if, the stakeholders continue to supply these services (conditionality), while beneficiary community members, water service providers and development partners are willing to pay for these ecosystem services.[235]

---

231 Shisanya, Luwesi and Obando, 2014
232 Porras, Aylward and Dengel, 2013
233 MEA, 2005
234 Smillie, and Helmich, 1999
235 Wunder, 2007

To translate such contractual arrangements into willingness to pay or to accept compensation for the delivery of ecosystem services, local stakeholders need to be convinced of the necessity of buying into the research findings on global changes and of embracing the water sector reforms.[236] Societal marketing management has thus been adopted in the water sector to mainstream commercial strategies for sales and promotion into communication, engagement and social behaviour change activities, such as raising awareness of compliance with public rules on drug abuse, smoking, sexual behaviour, taxes and other things.[237]

Societal marketing management usually focuses on knowledge acquisition, communication and engagement for uptake with various stakeholders targeted by the management, particularly the next and end users, in an attempt to get them to consider adopting relevant products (goods or services) suggested by the management.[238] Stakeholder engagement stimulates key stakeholders to buy into the management vision and missions, goals and targets through a partnership with, and participation of, these stakeholders in a reflection, persuasion and uptake process.[239] Through this process, managers get to grips with stakeholders' requirements, and measure their understanding and capacity to change. This enables strategies to be created that lead to the desired result or impact on the ground. This information is again fed into the reflection, persuasion and uptake process, in order to share progress made and results obtained with the stakeholders for appropriate responses, uptake and feedback.[240] Water managers are thus aware of emerging opportunities and threats arising from external stakeholders in the basin. They can thus make the appropriate responses, in the hope that, if properly engaged, the stakeholders will help create an environment conducive to the changes that the management hopes to achieve.[241]

## 5.2    Resolving the Deadlock through Reflection and Persuasion

There has been a breakdown in the communication between rural water resources management, and urban water supply on one side, and information, communication and persuasion for consumer behaviour change, on the other (Figure 5.1). Most rural communities and water users still believe that they have been abandoned by public governance and national development. They have no easy access to clean water and safe sanitation. Since they strive to acquire these resources by themselves, they strongly believe that no authority can charge them or tax them.[242] The slow pace of compliance with water use charges and water quality requirements is a major concern for water re-

---

236  Smith, Haugtvedt and Petty, 1994
237  Evans, 2006
238  Bamberg, Ajzen, and Schmidt, 2003
239  Petty and Cacioppo, 1986
240  Olson, 1965
241  WRMA. 2010
242  Förch, Winnegge, and Thiemann, 2010.

sources management boards and authorities across Africa – especially where awareness has been raised and agreement has been reached. It is disturbing overall implementation of the water sector reforms in Sub-Saharan Africa, owing to the reluctance and unwillingness on the part of water users to pay.[243] This explains the potential hostility and conflict between the water resources management and service authorities with their allies (the water users' associations and service boards), on one side, and private water service providers (companies) and community self-help groups (water systems and irrigation schemes), on the other.[244]

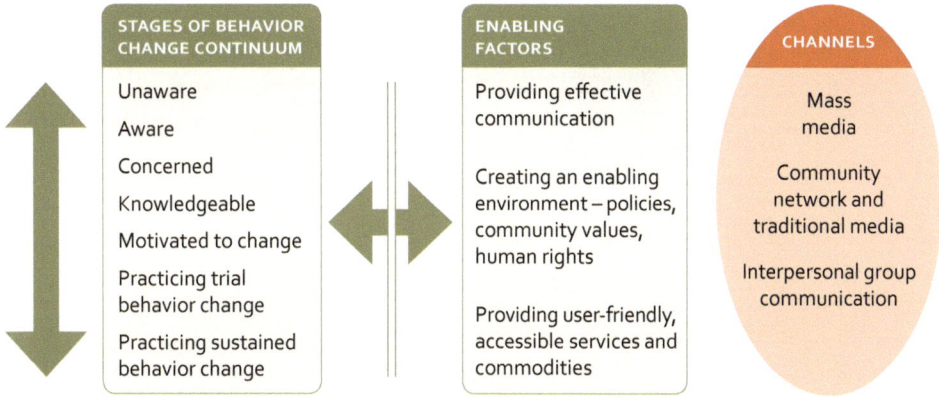

| STAGES OF BEHAVIOR CHANGE CONTINUUM | ENABLING FACTORS | CHANNELS |
|---|---|---|
| Unaware<br>Aware<br>Concerned<br>Knowledgeable<br>Motivated to change<br>Practicing trial behavior change<br>Practicing sustained behavior change | Providing effective communication<br><br>Creating an enabling environment – policies, community values, human rights<br><br>Providing user-friendly, accessible services and commodities | Mass media<br><br>Community network and traditional media<br><br>Interpersonal group communication |

**Figure 5.1.** The communication continuum in social marketing.[245]

To resolve the deadlock, most water management authorities and boards have decided to apply 'the stick' to enforce water laws. This has involved punitive measures, such as arresting and prosecuting illegal water users; handling water pumps, kiosks and irrigation schemes; and confiscating the equipment and tools used to draw water, especially during droughts.[246] However, these approaches have proved ineffective and unsustainable, as many stakeholders are often not keen on the reforms in place in the water sector. So necessity dictates a review of the approaches used by water authorities and boards towards enforcement of the 'user-pays' and 'polluter-pays' principles in the water sector, with a focus on societal marketing management.[247] This aims primarily at using advocacy and capacity-building approaches to entice local stakeholders on matters pertaining to integrated water resources management. Water board staff therefore need to be trained in methodologies to address perception and choice behaviour change, as well as promotion and communication.[248] However, the first step in this approach requires a situation analysis.

---

243  Nilsson, von Borgstede, and Biel, 2004
244  Mathenge, Luwesi, Shisanya, Mahiri, Akombo, Mutiso, 2014
245  Adapted after FHI, 2002
246  WRMA, 2010
247  K'akumu, 2008
248  Martinsen, 2008

## 5.2.1 Understanding the Reflection and Uptake Context

Societal marketing management suggests both tactical and strategic actions to be taken in the context of knowledge acquisition, management, communication, engagement and uptake to promote compliance with water use charges and effluent discharge fees.[249] The first step in achieving compliance is a situation analysis.[250] In marketing, the most frequently applied technique for situation analysis is known as SWOT analysis – short for Strengths, Weaknesses, Opportunities and Threats (Table 5.1).

| ENDOGENOUS FACTORS \ EXOGENOUS FACTORS | O External Opportunities | T External Threats |
|---|---|---|
| **S** Internal Strengths | **MAXIMAX STRATEGIES (S-O)** Strategies that use organisational strengths to take maximum advantage of environmental opportunities. | **MAXIMIN STRATEGIES (S-T)** Strategies that use organisational strengths to mitigate the impact of environmental threats. |
| **W** Internal Weaknesses | **MINIMAX STRATEGIES (W-O)** Strategies that minimize organisational weaknesses to take advantage of environmental opportunities. | **MINIMIN STRATEGIES (W-T)** Strategies that minimize organisational weaknesses to mitigate the impact of environmental threats. |

**Table 5.1.** A typical SWOT analysis matrix.[251]

SWOT analysis is a technique that assesses resources (internal strengths and external opportunities) to improve areas of competitive challenges (endogenous weaknesses and exogenous threats).[252] Strengths and weaknesses are structures and resources that contribute to the realization of management goals. Opportunities and threats are competitive outcomes encountered by the management from its interaction with its socio-political, economic and natural environments.[253]

## 5.2.2 Creating a Marketing Mix for Water Management

Water and sanitation suppliers often use different strategies from the proposed SWOT matrix to seek a specific planning mix or strategic assortment of marketing variables that will increase organizational resources through the transformation of weaknesses and threats into strengths and opportunities. To apply the suggested SWOT strategies, water services providers (WSPs) first seek to better understand their internal structures,

249  Hornik and Yanovitsky, 2003
250  US Department of Health and Human Services. 2010
251  Luwesi, Kinuthia, Mutiso, Akombo, Doke and Ruhakana, 2015
252  Bill and Strand, 2008
253  Scannell and Gifford, 2010

before they identify the needs and requirements, fears and expectations of water users, thus enabling them to design a marketing mix.[254] The most widely utilized marketing mix in the water sector is McCarthy's '4Ps', standing for P=Price; P=Product; P=Place; and P=Promotion.[255] This marketing mix determines the organization's position in the market through the quality of its goods or services (product), the price and promotional activities that induce water users' behaviour change for increased revenue.[256] Figure 5.2 presents a revised version of McCarthy's '4Ps' marketing mix.

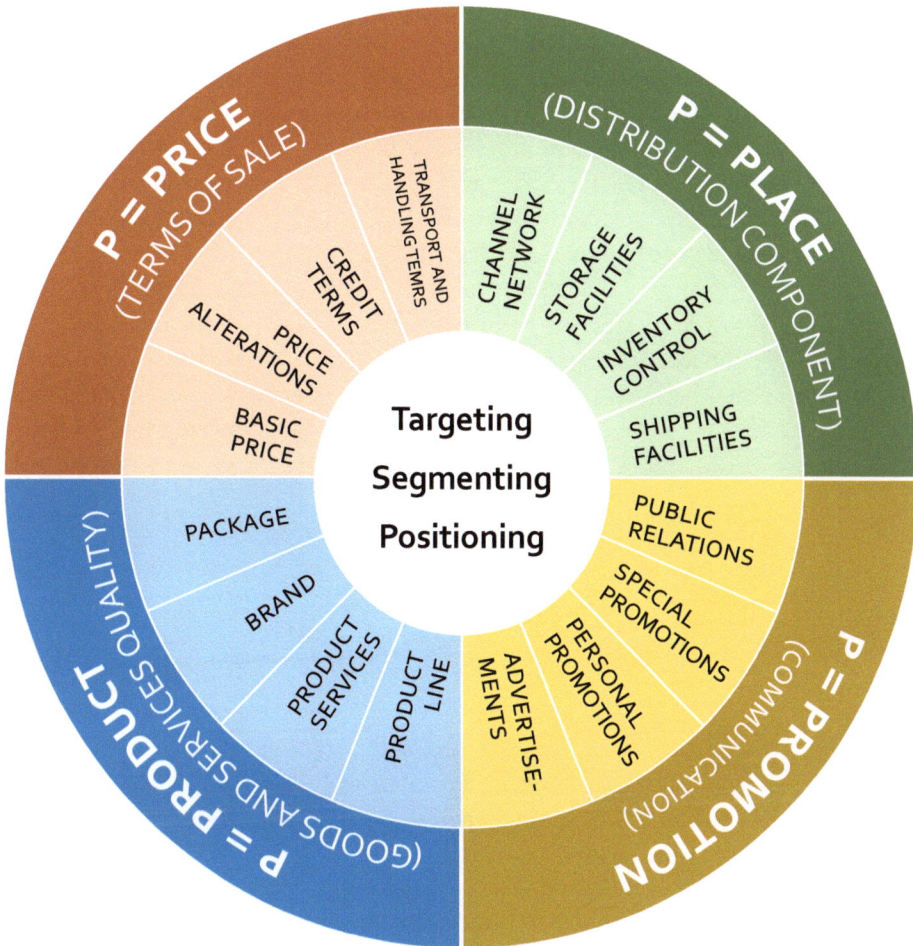

**Figure 5.2.** A revised version of McCarthy's '4Ps' marketing mix.[257]

254  Borden, 1964
255  Huhman, Heitzler and Wong, 2004
256  Andreasen, 1995
257  Adapted after Baker and Start, 1992

The mix of these four marketing variables (price, product, place and promotion) matches well with the supply strategy of most water and sanitation services' providers. However, when it comes to water resources management, which is a public service, this marketing management strategy may just compound three of the four components, the pricing of public services being generally predetermined by means of laws and decrees.[258]

### 5.2.3  Pricing Water Services

In Africa, the 'P' for price is generally a fee or a charge based on a tariff designed by a public utility; but in some cases, the price can be set by a private service provider to achieve full cost recovery. That is why, in most cases, public water supply is a state monopoly instituted by the rule of law. Where potable water is directly provided or is regulated by the state, price formation will not always be the result of market inter-actions between the suppliers and customers.[259] Frequently, water fees are arbitrary, determined on the basis of political motivations. In such a case, the service provider's bargaining power may not be adequate to allow income to cover expenditure (Figure 5.3). Thus, WSPs need efficient and productive methods to encourage behaviour change in water services pricing in order to attain full cost recovery. Nevertheless, agreement is needed between the private sector and the government to subsidize the cost difference for the development of water resources and other ecosystem services in the watershed.[260]

| | | Bargaining power / influence on people | |
| --- | --- | --- | --- |
| | | LOW | HIGH |
| Willingness to pay | HIGH | Cost of transaction + opportunity cost (full cost recovery) | Cost of transaction + shortage cost (arbitrary fee) |
| | LOW | Dumping fee (deficit) | Cost of transaction (subsidy) |

Figure 5.3. Price formation and bargaining outcomes in the water sector.[261]

The regulator of water services should take into consideration all the running costs of the service provider and the benefits to consumers, prior to setting the tariffs. This will enable the government to justify its water pricing policy.[262] Table 5.2 illustrates some benefits that accrue from water use charges and effluent discharge fees at various levels of implementation of water sector reforms. Water use charges and effluent discharge fees should be used to manage the water up to the end tap, and to generate higher profits through 'more crops per drop'. This means that water charges and fees should be

---

258  Kotler, 1991
259  Cunha,and Caldieraro, 2009
260  IUCN. 2016
261  Luwesi, 2011
262  WASREB, 2014

managed rationally for the benefit of both providers and users.[263] Implementing efficient water pricing would create an environment that is conducive to equitable water distribution. That, in turn, would enhance rational water use by local stakeholders in farming and other productive sectors. This would narrow the gap between upstream and downstream users, present and future generations. Water metering would help farmers and other water users to utilize their water resources efficiently and to manage their demand under the limits of their average costs and the minimum efficient scale of their production. Such efficient use of water resources would finally reduce water conflicts through the fair allocation of resources, particularly during periods of scarcity.[264]

| Levels of implementation: | | |
|---|---|---|
| **Household level** | **Firm/provider level** | **National level** |
| • Charges reduce domestic water cost through avoidance of waste (i.e. leakage, over-abstractions and overuse).<br><br>• They influence behaviour towards conservation and efficient water usage by future generations. | • Charges ensure cost recovery through the 'user-pays' principle.<br><br>• They constitute the cost factor in profit margin calculations.<br><br>• They influence the choice of production method and technology.<br><br>• They increase profitability through 'more yield per drop'.<br><br>• They also provide incentives for demand management.<br><br>• They signal consumer willingness to pay for additional investments in water services. | • Charges provide an income for subsidizing water projects to support disadvantaged groups and for funding watershed infrastructure and delivery of services for sustainability.<br><br>• They also allow equitable distribution of the resource.<br><br>• Effluent discharge fees are particularly a means for pollution control through the 'polluter-pays' principle.<br><br>• They provide incentives for watershed management. |

**Table 5.2.** Benefits accrue from payments for water use and effluent discharge.

## 5.2.4   Innovative Ways of Selling Water Products

The 'P' for product (good or service) refers primarily to the quality (contents, brands and water service lines) and quantity (capacity or storage) of water services and resources. The supply of any water service should be based on stakeholder needs. The product to be sold in the watershed would be an idea, practice, habit, belief, attitude and value that is appealing for the equitable distribution and conservation of water resources. It should also be a brand or a label that represents the benefits arising from private water provision and public intervention in a watershed, perhaps through technological innovation and safety support services.[265]

---

263  Barah, 2009
264  Luwesi, 2010
265  Evans, Price, and Blahut, 2005.

The 'P' for place stands for administrative distribution of private water services and different public interventions in the watershed. It includes the organization of water providers and users into specific physical entities (such as basins and sub-basins, catchments and sub-catchments) and social networks such as water industrialists, corporates and users' associations.[266] This would enable easy communication with the stakeholders on the process of supply of water services and the management of water resources. Watershed managers and water services providers should therefore cluster their stakeholders' expectations into groups of needs, within different watershed segments, to allow targeting of a leading support group.[267] For instance, one category of stakeholders would comprise farmers, distributors of farming inputs, water services providers, kiosk vendors and facilitators (brokers, transport, storage, financial lenders and advertisers). This would lead the manager to design a very special brand that would condition the mind of each member of the target social group.[268] As a result, the manager would successfully implement the watershed management plan in the cluster. Having the water service positioned in the mind of each stakeholder, the manager can take credit for having generated very valuable social capital for the organization.

### 5.2.5   Promoting Water Management and Services

The 'P' for promotion is the most important activity in any marketing mix. It encompasses public relations, promotional activities and advertising or publicity. Water managers need to use effective means of communication and engagement to create or re-create awareness of their services. They may also emphasize particular information pertaining to their service delivery.[269] Water managers are thus reminded to inform the public of how to apply a new regulation, where to find it, what specific features are to be retained and what changes have been made to previous legislation, as well as the potential effects that would result from application of the reforms.[270] If people are constantly reminded to change their behaviour, they are likely to develop favourable attitudes toward the water sector reforms. This may reinforce their determination to abide by the rules, so that they may enjoy immediate and future benefits accruing from the reforms. It could also initiate a permanent channel of communication that would induce loyalty to government agendas. And it could forge a lasting link in the minds of all stakeholders between the provision of private water services and the management of public water resources.[271] This would enable future generations to enjoy the same water resources as the current generation.

Water managers need to be very careful when designing their advertising and publicity. They should be keenly aware of their stakeholders' needs and requirements,

---

266  Luwesi, 2011
267  Biel and Thogersen, 2007
268  Aaker, 1996
269  McGregor, 2008
270  Carrus, Passafaro and Bonnes, 2008
271  Budescu, Broomell, and Por, 2009

fears and expectations. If there is any suspicion or criticism of the service accessibility and performance, charges and fees, tariffs and taxes, there should be a thorough examination of the complaint, prior to any communication or information being issued to the public.[272] Awareness of the problem or complaint should be clearly communicated through the mass media, advertising and other promotional efforts. Civil servants and staff from the WSPs should thus be available for personal engagement/interaction with customers and/or taxpayers.

To avoid any inconvenience, the message should be well conditioned to relate to the inner beliefs or values of the target group, in order to stimulate positive thoughts and quick response. It should also take account of experiences common to the public and of the various categories of needs in the catchment. That is to say, some people will be seeking satisfaction of their physiological needs, others will be yearning for safety, love and esteem and self-actualization: this is known as the Maslow scale of human needs.[273] Table 5.3 shows various ways in which a WSP or a public institution managing water resources could win the loyalty of its customers.

| MESSAGE FORMAT: | Goal | Scheduling | Media and vehicle mix | Target |
|---|---|---|---|---|
| **1. Dogmatic** | Convert or increase the number of adopters | Concentrated | Direct advertisement, TV, radio magazines, newspaper internet, SMS, forums, campaigns | Customers |
| **2. Emotional** | Attract new users | Continuous | TV, radio, social media, SMS, forums, campaigns | Gatekeepers |
| **3. Reason-giving** | Maintain user image | Intermittent | Direct advertisement, TV, radio magazines, newspaper, internet, SMS, forums, campaigns | Opinion leaders and others |
| **4. Factual / pragmatic** | Reinforce loyalty or attract new users | Intermittent | In situ demo, internet, social media, SMS, forums, campaigns | Any client |

**Table 5.3.** Communication and promotion strategy.[274]

Promotional activities should create or reinforce behaviours that are favourable to water rules and services, while discouraging unfavourable attitudes toward their adoption. However, the manager should avoid the post-dissonance effect on consumers' feelings. She needs to reinforce the conviction that the consumer has made the right choice or decision to pay for water services or to abide by the rules.[275] This may be done by packaging a number of support services known as 'customer care'. Table 5.4 illustrates various marketing models used to condition people's minds for effective consumer behaviour change.

---

272  Schultz, Nolan, Cialdini, Goldstein and Griskevicius, 2007
273  Carrus, Passafaro, and Bonnes, 2008
274  Adapted after Baker and Start, 1992
275  Schiffman, Kanuk, and Das, 2006

| MARKETING EFFECT: (CAC MODEL) | Strong's AIDA Model | Lavidge and Steiner Model | Rogers Model | Engel, Kollat and Blackwell Model |
|---|---|---|---|---|
| 1. Conative Effect (Motive) | • Action | • Purchase conviction | • Adoption<br>• Trial | • Purchase processes |
| 2. Affective Effect (Emotion) | • Desire<br>• Interest | • Preference<br>• Liking | • Evaluation<br>• Interest | • Evaluation and search |
| 3. Cognitive Effect (Thought) | • Awareness | • Knowledge<br>• Awareness<br>• Unawareness | • Awareness | • Problem recognition |

**Table 5.4.** Effects of marketing actions on consumers.[276]

If information on the product (goods or service) feeds back into its performance evaluation and a cost-benefit analysis, and if all of these are made available to the customer/taxpayer, that would reassure the taxpayer that paying water charges is beneficial to both his/her generation and future generations. That would progressively nurture his/her loyalty and moral integrity, when it comes to paying public duties or private service fees.[277] Yet loyalty comes into being, grows, matures and dies. Regular checks on compliance with rules and regulations governing private water services and public watershed management may provide information on the status of users' loyalty. Also, a long-term strategic action plan (SAP) is needed to coordinate efforts to maintain public relations, as well as to reduce public expenditure and recurring budget deficits.[278] The SAP would introduce a culture of behaviour change communication (BCC) that would strengthen the bond between government agencies, service providers and water users (Figure 5.4).

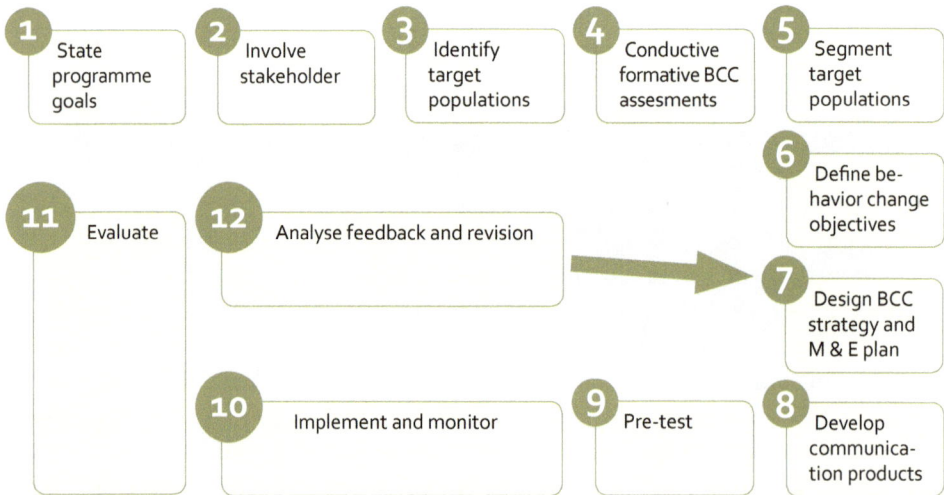

**Figure 5.4.** Framework for behaviour change communication culture(BCC).[279]

---

276  Adapted after Baker and Start, 1992; Hornik, 2002
277  Hornik and Yanovitsky, 2003
278  O'Sullivan, Yonkler, Morgan and Merritt, 2003
279  Adapted after FHI, 2002

### 5.2.6   Managing the Total Water Services Quality

Water sector actors are required to regularly conduct a total quality management (TQM) exercise, in order to assess the level of satisfaction of their customers. This enables them to provide efficient and effective services to their customers, and advances the bond between the state and private water actors.[280] Therefore, prior to adopting and implementing any marketing strategy, they should address the following concerns: (i) What do our customers want? (ii) What service do we provide? (iii) To what extent are customers satisfied? (iv) How can we improve what we offer? (v) What will this cost us and what benefits can we anticipate? Responses to these questions would form a basis for water services TQM.

Water services regulatory boards and resources management authorities, as well as companies and user groups, are advised to use bottom-up approaches to involve customers directly in policy-making, planning, implementation, coordination, monitoring and evaluation of water services and resources management. This requires a set of standards that ensure efficient and effective service delivery. It also demands effective communication tools and approaches for engaging key stakeholders.[281] The following section provides practical examples of such approaches and tools, building on the case of the 'CGIAR Research Programme on Water, Land and Ecosystems (WLE)'TM in the Volta and Niger basins, West Africa.

## 5.3   Societal Marketing in the Perspective of the CGIAR's Water, Land and Ecosystems Programme[282]

### 5.3.1   WLE Programme in the Volta and Niger Basins

The CGIAR's WLE research programme for the Volta and Niger basins envisioned sustainable management of the agro-ecological landscapes and ecological management systems to raise prosperity among smallholder farmers and provide food security to both rural and urban populations by the year 2025.[283] This can only be achieved through the strategic forging of partnerships in the region, to influence end and next users to generate and take up new knowledge, tools, methods and strategies, so as to build resilient institutions for future development and sustainable intensification of agriculture and pastoralism in different landscapes.[284] The programme performance depends on results-based management approaches oriented towards delivery of the expected development outcomes.

---

280  Carrus, Passafaro and Bonnes, 2008
281  Gardner and Stern, 2008
282  For more information visit the WLE websites: https://wle.cgiar.org ; https://cgspace.cgiar.org/
      handle/10568/34494 ; and, https://waterlandandecosystems.wikispaces.com/
283  WLE, 2015
284  Nicol, Langan, Victor and Gonsalves, 2015

The WLE research in the Volta and Niger basins revolves around three priority areas for achieving high impact. First, it aims at introducing innovative practices that would influence investments and interventions in sustainable agriculture and pastoralism intensification to cater for a growing population and to lead to greater food security and poverty reduction. Second, WLE targets increase productivity and sustainability of ecosystems and the services they provide in a sustainable and equitable way, particularly for women and youths. Third, this programme intends to influence governance and investment decision-making for scaling up (and scaling out) basin-level infrastructure to sustain and enhance ecosystem services, improve livelihoods and alleviate poverty.[285] To achieve these goals, WLE utilizes collaborative research activities with other think-tanks, beneficiary government agencies and communities (Figure 5.5). They get to study, share insights, knowledge and critical reflections on sustainable agricultural intensification within healthy watersheds, landscapes and ecosystems, using innovative approaches. The following sections elaborate on the communication and stakeholder engagement strategy, and looks at the diverse stakeholders that participated in the implementation of the 2015–16 programme.

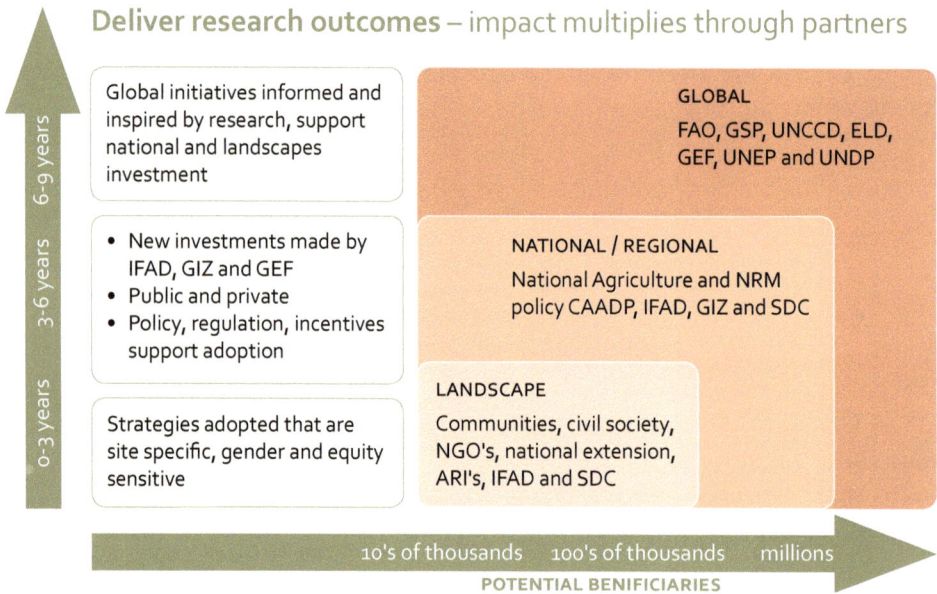

Figure 5.5. Partnership impact pathway for CGIAR's WLE programme in the Volta-Niger.[286]

### 5.3.2   Communication and Uptake Strategy

Communication is the most important activity of any corporate management, especially in the early stages of a programme life cycle. It enables stakeholders and partners to be constantly reminded that they need to change their behaviours in order to take

285  WLE, 2015a
286  Adapted from WLE. 2015b

up the necessary actions. Like commercial marketing, communication has aspects of public relations, advertising and promotional activities. The effective use of communication tools creates or re-creates awareness of the programme by informing stakeholders and partners about how to apply the new research findings, how to integrate them into policies, regulations and investments, and where to find them.[287]

The WLE strategy uses both traditional and modern communication and engagement approaches that are interdisciplinary, neutral and non-partisan, and that aim at creating synergies among different groups of stakeholders. Multi-stakeholder processes are used and backed with appropriate research results to foster the necessary policy and institutional changes. These processes involve clear stakeholder mapping and a variety of consultative engagements, lobbying and advocacy, and two-way dialogue between the programme management and the stakeholders.[288] Management regularly interacts with individuals, organizations and sectors through briefings when various milestones are attained during the implementation periods. Regular multi-stakeholder workshops and exchange visits with local researchers bring out opportunities and possible threats. These activities are closely monitored through process documentation and information gathered, and are subject to process analysis using social anthropological tools. The outcomes and lessons learned are communicated to stakeholders, and later fed into innovative research programmes and adaptive management.[289]

### 5.3.3   Stakeholder Analysis

The programme targets next and end users of research products, including policy-makers and investors, as well as community members, development partners and any other person or institution capable of influencing the implementation of research recommendations. These stakeholders are engaged at three levels: the regional (basin-wide), national and local levels. Policy-makers and investors are engaged from the beginning of the programme, so that researchers can align their research objectives to take account of policy requirements and targets, internal and external contexts, opportunities for the implementation of research recommendations by end users and feedback from these end users to researchers.[290]

Government agencies: WLE aligns its objectives and activities with the priorities of government ministries and departments. These are included in the projects, so that they can contribute to the design and development of ecosystem-based concepts (knowledge and tools), as well as approaches that need to be applied in planning and investment decisions to improve the livelihoods of vulnerable communities, while ensuring sustained environmental health.

Government ministries and departments in Burkina Faso, Ghana, Mali and Niger are specifically targeted to get them to use the new knowledge about biomass manage-

---

287  C-Change. 2012
288  Smillie, and Helmich, 1999.
289  Uiterkamp, and Vlek, 2007
290  Stein, Barron, Nigussie, Gedif, Amsalu and Langan, 2013

ment in mixed crop livestock and agro-ecological landscapes. Such an informed policy and development formulation is likely to improve livelihoods for men, women and youth through agriculture and livestock intensification in healthy ecosystems. Training modules based on project results are also planned for agriculture and district government training institutes.[291]

Development organizations: International development organizations are provided with briefs, e-newsletters, wiki/blog posts, engagement journals, process documentation and other tools to help them target and prioritize ecosystem-based interventions. Both ecologically and economically sustainable investments are targeted in an effort to improve food security, nutrition and livelihoods of rural communities and provide employment opportunities to young people. These may constitute true motivations for people to change their life styles in the course of climate change.[292]

Local institutions: local institutions acquire new knowledge, methods and frameworks for governing ecosystem services in the collective management of their farming landscape. During the planning and implementation processes, local governments and other partners directly involved in projects taking place in Burkina Faso, Ghana, Mali and Niger were trained to use evidence-based knowledge on economic valuation of ecosystem services; and the cost-effectiveness and impacts of sustainable land management (SLM) and ecosystems-based management (EBM).[293]

The private sector business community makes an informed investment decision based on the results of feasibility studies on agricultural investments, which are in line with the WLE vision of sustainable intensification and ecosystem services resilience. For instance, the resource, recovery and reuse (RRR) research project in Ghana keeps disseminating the 'fortifer' bio-fertilizer, based on faecal sludge, that was developed in 2010 by its researchers. A fertilizer plant is being built to serve specific clients in West Africa, particularly in Northern Ghana and Southern Burkina Faso.[294]

Community members are empowered to engage with decision-makers through participatory platforms and existing forums. For example, the integrated crop-livestock farm communities and related biomass value-chain actors have adopted gender and youth-sensitive farming practices. This is likely to enhance biomass productivity and improve the sustainability of land and water resources across agro-ecological landscapes, by providing, supporting and regulating ecosystem services in the Sahelian landscapes of Burkina Faso, Mali and Niger. It would also enable women and young people to benefit in both the short and the long term from EBM and SLM approaches.[295]

291  Sidibé and Williams, 2016
292  APA-Force on Climate Change, 2009
293  Williams, Mul, Biney and Smakhtin, 2016
294  IUCN, 2016
295  Dunlap, Van Liere, Mertig and Jones, 2000

### 5.3.4  Planning for Communication and Uptake Activities

Once stakeholders and partners are well known, prior to engaging them in any communication and uptake activity, the following concerns should be addressed:

- What do our stakeholders and partners want?
- What service can we provide to them to achieve our objectives?
- Who do we need to meet, where and when?
- What will be our message?
- For the various activities, who will be part of the platform?
- Is there any existing platform to link to without necessarily starting something new?
- Do we have enough capability (data/information, manpower) to influence policy and decision-making processes?
- Where are there more opportunities for influencing policy/decision-makers?
- What will this cost us and what benefits can we anticipate?
- Who can we target as national/regional facilitator for continuous engagement with stakeholders?
- When can we be assured that our customers are satisfied?
- How can we improve what we offer?

Responses to these questions form a basis for water, land and ecosystems TQM. It is advisable to use bottom-up approaches, in order to involve all stakeholders directly in research and the implementation of research recommendations for investments, policy-making, planning, implementation, coordination, monitoring and evaluation.[296] This will be a standard for efficient and effective communication and engagement for WLE research projects service delivery in the Volta and Niger basins.

### 5.3.5  Communication Approaches for Catalysing Research Uptake

Stakeholders need at all times to be aware of how a programme is performing. WLE developed innovative communication approaches tailored to the needs and requirements of its stakeholders. It keeps their fidelity by incorporating their fears and expectations into the messaging format of any promotional activity.[297] The following steps are followed closely when designing communication and engagement methods to involve stakeholders and partners:

i.   Start with sharing a package of the recent results of the programme (phase I: 2008–2016);

ii.  Talk to them about WLE programme phase II (2016–2022) and listen to their feedback;

---

296  Porras, Aylward and Dengel, 2013
297  Moser, 2007

iii. Keep them informed subsequently;

iv. Organize periodic consultative meetings which could be of diverse forms: informal one-on-one meetings, consultative sessions and discussion/presentations at special events.

Table 5.5 illustrates how communication and engagement activities are adapted to the target audiences.

| Service | How | Tools | Audiences |
|---|---|---|---|
| Messaging | Hone and define messages in ways that can be communicated externally | e-newsletters; media kits | Donors, partners, policy-makers, communities |
| Participatory video | Sharing and exchanging knowledge | Video production | Within communities, policy-makers |
| Storytelling | Discuss starting points that show facts or realities from the field for common understanding (no technical jargon) | Video, audio interview, photo stories, blog | Policy-makers, stakeholders, donors |
| Media | Scaling messages, engaging with different stakeholders, reaching audiences using accessible tools | Radio, print, TV | Donors, government officials, communities, extension agents |
| Websites | Assess needs for websites; search for regional data portals to target specific audiences; present data and models on open access websites | Data management systems, open access tools | Donors, research users |
| Repackaging research | Break science down into layman language and understandable pieces, e.g. using animation, comics | Technical briefs, policy briefs, infographics, sourcebooks, games | Policy-makers, other scientists, extension agents, regional planners, students/educators |
| Social Media | Broadcast messages and event engagement; engage with the general public and create awareness | Twitter, Facebook, LinkedIn, Yammer, etc. | Students, researchers, donors, partners, general public |

**Table 5.5.** Communication and engagement activities for specific audiences.[298]

The management of WLE in the Volta and Niger basins has resolved to be active in interacting and engaging with policy-makers and investors. In general, implementation of the strategy comprises four levels: coordination; engagement and outreach; communication; and knowledge sharing.[299] The regional manager for the area concerned

298 WLE, 2015c
299 WLE, 2015a

is in complete charge of coordinating implementation of the strategy at the regional level, through monthly meetings and one-on-one interactions with key stakeholders and partners. The remaining activities are mainly implemented by project leaders and opinion leaders from the region (Volta and Niger basins) and countries involved in the strategy (i.e. Burkina Faso, Ghana, Mali and Niger). The focal region projects simply support and incorporate these strategies in their communication and engagement activities.

To ensure coordination of the programme, the manager invites different stakeholders to various forums.[300] These include outreach discussions (ORD), basin-wide dialogues (BWD), basin-wide business forums (BWBF), end-of-programme seminars and conferences (EPSC), training workshops, joint proposal writeshops (JPW), electronic messaging (EMS) and social media (SM). Using canvassing methods, ORD meetings are used to approach investors, policy-makers and donors at their place of work on key issues pertaining to the integration of ecosystem solutions into policy and investments. BWDs are held annually in a selected country (i.e. Burkina Faso, Ghana, Mali or Niger) in order to showcase the progress already made and demonstrate what remains to be achieved. Where there is a great need to engage with end users, the BWBFs are occasionally designed to inform potential investors about some of the business opportunities offered to them by WLE based on research results. The EPSC may be a milestone in disseminating the programme's achievements among key stakeholders and next users. The congress may culminate with the compilation of a sourcebook on sustainable policies and investments in agriculture. EMS – such as e-newsletters, wikis, blog posts, podcasts, video conferencing, engagement journals, process documentation, etc. – allows partners to be reached at any time. Finally, JPWs enable funds to be sourced together with local stakeholders and/or partners outside the region.

National consultative forums are mainly designed for policy-makers and the business community. During Phase 1 of the programme implementation, they were planned for the first and second quarters of 2016. The preparation included rigorous one-on-one consultations using canvassing as the main communication and engagement strategy. Key themes addressed during the consultations included: (i) investments for water-smart agriculture (WSA); (ii) ecologically viable options for agriculture intensification; (iii) agroforestry and soil conservation intensification for food production; (iv) investments for agricultural water development; and (v) integrating watershed management and community engagement in agricultural policies and investments.[301]

After assessing the progress of the WLE programme in West Africa, it appears that most projects were mainly funded by global agencies such as IFAD, DfID and USAID in 2015 and 2016. The focal region management has carefully monitored and evaluated the implementation of these research activities and their outcomes on vulnerable rural communities. The management played a key role in coordinating the involvement of research partners from public and global policy institutions, as well as from

---

300  WLE, 2015b
301  Luwesi and Cofie, 2015

**The Niger and Volta Basins**

☐ The Niger Basin (2.27 million km²)
☐ The Volta Basin (0.39 million km²)

*Source: Adapted from CGIAR (2015)*

**Map 5.1.** With a length of 4,200 km, the Niger River is the third longest river in Africa after the Nile and the Congo River. The Niger traverses four countries, its basin covers 2.27 million km² and is shared by ten countries – Algeria, Benin, Burkina Faso, Cameroon, Chad, Côte d'Ivoire, Guinea, Mali, Niger and Nigeria. The Volta river is 1,600 km long and its catchment area covers 394,000 km² distributed between Burkina Faso, Ghana, Togo, Mali, Benin and Cote d'Ivoire. Source: African Partnerships for Sustainable Growth, FIDIC GAMA 2017.

academia, in research to help local stakeholders improve their management of water resources in the Volta and the Niger basins. Innovative ways of managing ecosystems have been unveiled to overcome a changing climate and thus curb its threats to agriculture and food security in West Africa. After receiving feedback from stakeholders on the ongoing research activities, WLE management proceeded to the revision of its programme outcomes to fit with the priorities of local communities and governments.

This final process consisted mainly of identifying gaps that needed to be addressed during the next phase of WLE implementation to provide a platform for engagement with regional stakeholders. After discussions with project partners, links between WLE projects and partner initiatives going on in the region were identified. An assessment of their potential contribution to the development outcomes of WLE in the region was conducted to help revise WLE research activities and set new targets for the projects. Research on water, land and agro-ecosystems management is indeed worth encouraging, if food security and economic development are to be achieved in the West African region.

## 5.4    Conclusion

Local stakeholders have been slow to embrace the water sector reforms in many African countries, and this has cost vast sums in lost revenue and tax money. One main reason has been the ineffective use of promotional tools for communication and outreach and lack of uptake of the reforms by water authorities. This chapter has emphasized the need for social mobilization and advocacy, alongside promotional activities and publicity, as means of translating research findings into decision-making and of attracting local stakeholders to buy into and embrace water sector reforms. Water managers should therefore consider more communication and networking tools in order to disseminate their programmes and products. They are constantly reminded to be more persuasive when enforcing 'user-pays' and 'polluter-pays' principles. Such methods are likely to lead their stakeholders and partners to a positive change in their attitudes and the expected management outcomes.

A strategy for communication, engagement and outreach is crucial not only for informing the public of the activities being undertaken, but also for getting stakeholders to buy into the reforms and to support uptake as next users. Therefore, the management needs to plan carefully 'what' and 'how' it tells the public about its performance, using specific messaging tactics. Social mobilization and advocacy is expected to encourage key stakeholders to take the actions needed for uptake of research outputs. A promotional tactic that focuses on publicity would inform and educate them to make informed decisions for crucial uptake. It is recommended that water services providers and watershed managers take account of the prevailing environment and use their insight when enforcing water use charges/pollution discharge fees, tariffs, taxes or penalties to facilitate smooth achievement of the water sector outcomes. Only if the local stakeholders adhere to the reforms will those responsible for the funding be motivated to finance the various activities stipulated under the water sector strategies and plans; only then will water governance performance become a reality. This would help create the necessary values for the goals and outcomes of the water sector reforms to be attained in most African countries.

# References

Aaker D. 1996. Building strong brands. New York, NY: Simon and Schuster.

Andreasen A. 1995. Social change. San Francisco, CA: Jossey-Bass.

APA Task Force on Climate Change [American Psychological Association Task Force on the Interface Between Psychology and Global Climate Change]. 2009. Psychology and global climate change: Addressing a multi-faceted phenomenon and set of challenges. Available at: http://www.apa.org/science/about/publications/climate-change.aspx (Accessed on 11.02.2010).

Bamberg, S., Ajzen, I. and Schmidt, P. 2003. Choice of travel mode in the theory of planned behavior: The roles of past behavior, habit and reasoned action. Basic and Applied Social Psychology, 25: 175–187.

Barah, B.C. 2009. Economic and ecological benefits of system of rice intensification (SRI) in Tamil Nadu. Agricultural Economics Research Review, Vol. 22 (July-December 2009): 209-214.

Biel, A., and Thogersen, J. 2007. Activation of social norms in social dilemmas: A review of the evidence and reflections on the implications for environmental behavior. Journal of Economic Psychology, 28, 93–112.

Bill, S. and Strand, J. 2008. Social Marketing Behavior: A Practical Resource for Social Change Professionals. Washington, DC: AED.

Borden, N. 1964. The concept of the marketing mix. J Advertis Res 4: 2-7.

Budescu, D.V., Broomell, S., and Por, H.H. 2009. Improving communication of uncertainty in the reports of the Intergovernmental Panel on Climate Change. Psychological Science, 20: 299–308.

Carrus, G., Passafaro, P., and Bonnes, M. 2008. Emotions, habits and rational choices in ecological behaviours: The case of recycling and use of public transportation. Journal of Environmental Psychology, 28, 51– 62.

C-Change. [Communication for Change]. 2012. C-Bulletins: Developing and Adapting Materials for Audiences with Lower Literacy Skills. Washington, DC: FHI.360/C-Change.

Cunha, M., Jr., and Caldieraro, F. 2009. Sunk-cost effects on purely behavioral investments. Cognitive Science: A Multidisciplinary Journal, 33: 105–113.

Dunlap, R.E., Van Liere, K.D., Mertig, A.G., and Jones, R.E. 2000. Measuring endorsement of the new ecological paradigm: A revised NEP scale. Journal of Social Issues, 56, 425–442.

Evans, D., Price, S. and Blahut, S. 2005. Evaluating the TRUTH brand. J Health Commun. 10: 181-92

Evans, W.D. 2006. How social marketing works in health care. BMJ. 332(7551): 1207–1210.

FHI. [Family Health International Institute for HIV/AIDS]. 2002. Behavior change communication (BCC) for HIV/AIDS : a strategic framework. Arlington, VA: USAID IMPACT Project. Available at: http://www.hivpolicy.org/Library/HPP000533.pdf (Accessed on 12.03.2010).

Förch, G., Winnegge, R. and Thiemann, S. (Eds). 2010. DAAD Alumni Summer School: Financial instruments for integrated watershed management .Final Report. CICD Series No 9. Siegen: Universität Siegen.

Gardner, G.T., and Stern, P.C. 2008. The short list: The most effective actions U.S. households can take to curb climate change. Environment, 12–25.

Hornik, R. and Yanovitsky, I. 2003. Using theory to design evaluations of communication campaigns: the case of the national youth anti-drug media campaign. Commun Theory;13: 204-24.

Hornik, R.C. 2002. Public health communication: evidence for behavior change. Mahwah, NJ: Erlbaum,

Huhman, M., Heitzler, C., Wong, F. 2004. The VERB campaign logic model: a tool for planning and evaluation. Prev Chronic Dis;1(3): A11.

IUCN [International Union for Conservation of Nature]. 2016. Knowledge for SDG Action in West Asia and North Africa: R-KNOW Water Governance Best Practices within the Water, Energy,Food and Climate Change Nexus. Amman: IUCN- Regional Office for West Asia. Available at: www.iucn.org/westasia (Accessed on 06.03.2017).

K'akumu, O.A. 2008. Mainstreaming the participatory approach in water resource governance: The 2002 water law in Kenya. Development 51: 56-62.

Kotler, P. 1991. Marketing Management: Analysis, Planning and Control, 8th Ed.. Englewoods Cliffs, N.J.: Prentice-Hall.

Luwesi, C.N. (Ed.). 2011. Innovative Ways in Financing the Water Sector. Final SWAP/bfz Workshop Report. Mombasa: Bfz and WaterCap, 7-11 November 2011. Available at: http://www.swap-bfz.org/Publications/financing_water_infrastructure.pdf (Accessed on 17.03.2013).

Luwesi, C.N. 2010. Hydro-economic Inventory in Changing Environment – An assessment of the efficiency of farming water demand under fluctuating rainfall regimes in semi-arid lands of South-East Kenya. Saarbrüken: Lambert Academic Publishing.

Luwesi, C.N. and Cofie, O. 2015. Transboundary challenges and opportunities in the Volta basin. Paper presented during CGIAR-WLE Greater Mekong Forum on Water, Food and Energy. 21-23 Oct. 2015. Phnom Penh: Cambodiana Hotel.

Luwesi, C.N., Kinuthia, W., Mutiso, M.N., Akombo, R.A., Doke, D.A. and Ruhakana, A. 2015. Climate Change, Pro-Poor Schemes and Water Inequality - Strengths and Weaknesses of Kauti Irrigation Water Users' Association, Kenya. In: A. Beyene (Ed.), Agricultural Water Institutions in East Africa. Nordiska Afrikainstitutet, Uppsala, Current African Issues 63: 43 – 60.

Martinsen C. 2008. Social marketing in sanitation- More than selling toilets. Stockholm Water Front, No1 (April 2008): 14-16.

Mathenge, J.M., Luwesi, C.N., Shisanya, C.A., Mahiri, I., Akombo, R.A., Mutiso, M.N. 2014. Water Security Where Governmental Policies Conflict with Local Practices: The Roles of Community Water Management Systems in Ngaciuma-Kinyaritha, Kenya. International Journal of Innovative Research and Development (IJIRD), Vol. 3 (5): 793-804.

McGregor, S.L.T. 2008. Conceptualizing immoral and unethical consumption using neutralization theory. Family and Consumer Sciences Research Journal, 36, 261–276.

MEA [Millennium Ecosystem Assessment]. 2005. Ecosystems and Human Well-being: Synthesis. Washington, DC.: World Resources Institute (WRI), Island Press.

Moser, S.C. 2007. More bad news: The risk of neglecting emotional responses to climate change information. In S.C. Moser and L. Dilling (Eds.), Creating a climate for change. New York, NY: Cambridge University Press.

Nicol, A.; Langan, S.; Victor, M.; Gonsalves, J. (Eds.) 2015. Water-smart agriculture in East Africa. Colombo: International Water Management Institute (IWMI). CGIAR Research Program on Water, Land and Ecosystems (WLE); and - Kampala: Global Water Initiative East Africa (GWI EA) Available at: https://cgspace.cgiar.org/handle/10568/64962 (Accessed on 12.05.2016).

Nilsson, A., von Borgstede, C. and Biel, A. 2004. Willingness to accept climate change strategies: The effect of values and norms. Journal of Environmental Psychology, 24, 267–277.

O'Sullivan, G., Yonkler, J., Morgan, W. and Merritt, A.P.. 2003. A field guide to designing a health communication strategy. Baltimore, MD: Johns Hopkins.

Olson, M.L., Jr. 1965. The logic of collective action: Public goods and the theory of groups. Cambridge, MA: Harvard University Press.

Petty R.E, and Cacioppo J.T. 1986. Communication and persuasion: central and peripheral routes to attitude change. New York: Springer-Verlag.

Porras, I., Aylward, B. and Dengel, J. 2013. Monitoring payments for watershed services schemes in developing countries. London: International Institute for Environment and Development (IIED), Sustainable Markets Group.

Scannell, L., and Gifford, R. 2010. The relations between natural and civic place attachment and pro-environmental behavior. Journal of Environmental Psychology, 30: 289 –297.

Schiffman, L.G., Kanuk, L.L., and Das, M. 2006. Consumer behaviour. Toronto, ON: Pearson Education.

Schultz, P.W., Nolan, J.M., Cialdini, R.B., Goldstein, N.J., and Griskevicius, V. 2007. The constructive, destructive, and reconstructive power of social norms. Psychological Science, 18, 429 – 434.

Shisanya, C.A., Luwesi, C.N. and Obando, J.A. 2014. Innovative but Not Feasible: Green Water Saving Schemes at the Crossroad in Semi-Arid Lands. In: P. Chanie (ed.), Innovative Water Resource Use and Management for Poverty Reduction in Sub-Saharan Africa: An Anthology. Addis Ababa: OSSREA, pp. 137-172.

Sidibé, Y. and Williams, T.O. 2016. Agricultural land investments and water management in the Office du Niger, Mali: Options for improved water pricing. Water International 41 (5): 738-755.

Smillie, I and Helmich, H. (Eds.). 1999. Stakeholders: Government–NGO partnerships for international development. London: Earthscan.

Smillie, I. and Helmich, H. (Eds.). 1999. Stakeholders: Government–NGO partnerships for international development. London: Earthscan.

Smith, S.M., Haugtvedt, C.P., and Petty, R.E. 1994. Attitudes and recycling: Does the measurement of affect enhance behavioral prediction? Psychology and Marketing, 11, 359 –374.

Stein, C., Barron, J., Nigussie, L., Gedif, B., Amsalu, T. and Langan, S. 2013. Advancing the Water-energy-food Nexus: Social Networks and Institutional Interplay in the Blue Nile. Colombo: CGIAR Research Program on Water, Land and Ecosystems (WLE), Research for Development (R4d) Learning Series 2.

Uiterkamp, A.J.M.S. and Vlek, C. 2007. Practice and outcomes of multidisciplinary research for environmental sustainability. Journal of Social Issues, 63: 175–197.

US Department of Health and Human Services. 2010. Healthy people 2010: understanding and improving health. 2nd ed. Washington, DC: US Government Printing Office.

WASREB [Water Services Regulatory Board]. 2014. Assessing options to achieve commercial viability and financial sustainability of water supply and sanitation services. Nairobi: German Cooperation (GiZ).

WLE [CGIAR Research Program on Water, Land and Ecosystems]. (WLE). WLE websites Available at: https://wle.cgiar.org ; https://cgspace.cgiar.org/handle/10568/34494 ; and, https://waterlandandecosystems.wikispaces.com/

WLE [CGIAR Research Program on Water, Land and Ecosystems]. 2015a. WLE Focal region program brief: WLE Volta-Niger. Available at: https://cgspace.cgiar.org/bitstream/handle/10568/68827/WLE%20Focal%20region%20program%20brief_Volta_low%20res.pdf?sequence=1&isAllowed=y (Accessed on 12.05.2016)

WLE. [CGIAR Research Program on Water, Land and Ecosystems]. 2015b. Water, land and ecosystem in Africa (WLE in Africa): 2015 project review and stakeholder engagement workshop report held from 15-17 June 2015 in Ouagadougou, Burkina Faso. Available at: https://waterlandandecosystems.wikispaces.com/ (Accessed on 12.05.2016).

WLE [CGIAR Research Program on Water, Land and Ecosystems]. 2015c. WLE Volta-Niger Communication Engagement and outreach strategy and plan 2015-2016 (Unpublished Internal Document).

WRMA [Water Resources Management Authority]. 2010. Enforcement of Water Use Charges and Water Quality Thresholds in Kenya. WRMA Evaluation Workshop. Meru: Kenyatta University and the University of Siegen.

Williams, T.O.; Mul, M.L.; Biney, C.A.; Smakhtin, V. (Eds.) 2016. The Volta River Basin: Water for food, economic growth and environment. London: Routledge, Taylor & Francis Group.

Wunder, S. 2007. The efficiency of payments for environmental services in tropical conservation. Conservation Biology 21 (1): 48-58.

> Globally women have been identified as controlling over 70 percent of household spending decisions.

Anne Marie Tiani, senior scientist at the
Center for International Forestry (CIFOR),
conducts a workshop on climate change
in Lukolela, Democratic Republic of Congo.
Photo credit Ollivier Girard, CIFOR

# CHAPTER 6 Summary

- WATER COMPANIES AND INSTITUTIONS should draw on women's groups; taking account of their inner beliefs and values, their perceptions and choice behaviours, their expectations and fears, they should entrust women with financial management.
- WATER COMPANIES AND INSTITUTIONS should execute an about-turn in finance by channelling women's art and skill in safeguarding the treasury to increase institutional trustworthiness, and in communication to mobilize more funds through public relations, sales, promotional activities and publicity.
- IMPLEMENTATION of the 'women in water finance' concept should stimulate a quick response to exploiting women's talents in strategic financial management, communication and engagement, sales and marketing, and treasury safeguarding.
- IMPLEMENTATION of the 'women in water finance' concept will ease the severe pressure created by government budget deficits in the water sector, which no longer allow subsidies for water tariffs and sanitation services or guarantee borrowing.
- MAINSTREAMING THIS NEW PARADIGM will reinforce the public conviction that women are well suited to finance and other management positions.

Chapter 6:

# Gender in Water Finance: Perspectives for a Paradigm Shift in Water Finance Management

*Elsie Odonkor, Linnet Hamasi, Florence Muthoni, Mathabo Khau and Mary Mutiso*

## 6.1    Introduction

Recognition of the interdependence of gender and water has influenced the international development agenda for some time. This has led to international and national policy statements that urge and pledge support for 'mainstreaming gender' in the water sector.[302] Although there are some variations, the broad themes of these international and national policies are expressed in the Guiding Principles of the 1992 Dublin Conference on Water and the Environment.[303] The Dublin principle identified four major pillars in water management. It calls for a holistic view of water resources management (WRM) that combines social, economic and environmental considerations, and that recognizes the multiple uses of water. Thus, proceeding from the Dublin principle, it is imperative for water resources to be managed holistically and in a participatory manner, not underplaying the key role that women play in the provision and management of water or the economic value of water.[304]

In the context of implementation of these integrated water management policies, programmes and strategies, previous studies have highlighted women's involvement and engagement in some planning and management meetings.[305] Thanks to their reproductive and productive use of water, women have a lot to offer in terms of water resources management, and their role has been less than outstanding. A UN-Water survey of 40 African countries, compiled by the African Ministers' Council on Water (AMCOW), shows that the issue of sustainable water financing for water development in Africa has been a challenge for most governments. The issue was considered central to the ability of African governments to deliver on the Millennium Development

---

302  IRC, 2004
303  Cleaver, 1998
304  Solanes and Gonzalez-Villarreal,1999
305  IRC, 2004

Goals (MDGs) and later on the Sustainable Development Goals (SDGs) for water and sanitation, as well as to build the necessary infrastructure for economic development.[306] Achieving sustainability in financing will likely require some form of cost recovery from those who use the water resources on a business scale. AMCOW thus proposes investigating the collection, storage and analysis of financial data on water investment and WRM, in order to improve the water sector.[307] This can be achieved if there is increased involvement of users in the management of water resources through increased payments and participatory approaches that recognize the central role of women.[308]

However, in many African communities, the patriarchal gender order has made it such that women have had several stereotypical gender roles and assumptions blocking their capabilities within leadership and management roles. Patriarchy's legacy has been that men are seen as leaders and decision-makers in the public sphere, while women are relegated to the private sphere of the home as nurturers and caregivers who are not capable of public decision-making.[309] Despite the advances that have been made to redress the gendered inequalities that suppress women, there are still some arenas in which women's representation and contributions are minimal due to the gendered constructions of manhood and womanhood.[310] Addressing the gendered power dynamics within such spheres could create opportunities for women's agency to be enabled by providing the resources necessary for them to explore their capabilities towards economic and social justice.

Therefore, this chapter employs some African sayings, commonly used in East, Central and West Africa, to look at the roles that women can play in securing sustainable water financing in the continent. These include adages such as 'Women do not leave anything to chance' (strategic management), 'Women talk a lot' (communication and engagement ability), 'Women buy and sell everything they find on their way' (sales and marketing ability), 'Women are afraid of money' (treasury safeguarding ability). Prior to analysing these narratives, a theoretical framework is presented to contextualize the need for a paradigm shift.

## 6.2 Theory of Change for Innovative Water Finance

The main concern of this chapter is to understand how the involvement of women in water finance may have positive effects or boost innovations in water finance in Africa. To solve this problem, we need first of all to interrogate the processes and mechanisms that limit change in the behaviour of water sector agents to embrace a gender-based approach in the world of business. Thus, this chapter needed a strong theoretical background supporting this 'paradigm shift'. In this regard, we have selected four major

---

306  AMCOW, 2012
307  AMCOW, 2012
308  Clever, 1998
309  Connell, 2002; 2005
310  Morrell et al., 2009

theories that explain the push and pull factors that would boost women's leadership in water finance and enable accrual of resources in the water sector. These include Mullen and Johnson (1990) 'narrative theory',[311] Bourdieu (1992) 'logic of practice theory',[312] Gurian and Annis (2008) 'gender polarity theory'[313] and Burke (1966) 'behaviour change theory'.[314]

The first theory is from Mullen and Johnson (1990), which focuses on women's rhetoric and stereotyping, and is known as the 'narrative theory'. This theory explains that stories of women leaders rely on stereotypes to persuade their audience. The media and communities have therefore created narratives that portray women's leadership and empowerment as a deviation from the accepted norms.[315] How the other male members of the community view women leaders is clearly engraved in this victimhood framework, which presents them as outcasts and deviants, rather than heroes and achievers. The media and society created this framework in order to maintain loyalty to chauvinistic narratives, such as 'women should be submissive to men'; 'women should never look down on men'; 'women should feel like women'; 'it takes a woman to understand what a woman means'. These narratives have made the superstructure of most collapsing businesses, which have ignored women's potential in financial planning, management and communication for long. Are women taking advantage of these stereotypes to access leadership and perform better than their male counterparts? Or are they reacting to the silences that these stereotypes have created around them? Is leadership in water finance management a better means for women to get noticed in the water sector, or is it a reconstruction of patriarchy for more inclusive societies? Or simply a misinterpretation of feminism and/or influence of human rights-based approach? The answers to these questions provide the different motivations for a paradigm shift in water finance management.

The second theory is borrowed from Bourdieu (1992) and is known as 'logic of practice' theory. It suggests that subjects modify and transform social practices through their activity to give meaning to their lives through interaction between contexts and the social actions that are practised within those spaces (Webb et al., 2002).[316] This interaction relies on three major socio-cultural and economic resources: namely capital, field and habitus. Hence, women use their capital or the resources they gain through social and cultural networks and social positions (field). Using this social and cultural heritage, habits and social networks (habitus), they are able to translate their relationships into physical or economic capital (e.g. finance). They may also act as agents in the reconstruction and transformation of societies, social practices and institutions. Therefore, we cannot have 'social change' (i.e. financing boost) 'outside the action of the subjects' (i.e. women). Hence women's involvement in water finance may modify and

---

311  Mullen and Johnson, 1990
312  Bourdieu, 1992
313  Gurian and Annis, 2008
314  Burke, 1966
315  Haraway, 1990; Hodgson and McCurdy, 2001; Biel and Thogersen, 2007
316  Webb, Schirato and Danaher, 2002

transform social practices and therefore needs to be constituted within and by the practice of water finance management in which they participate. The first step towards such a 'paradigm shift' should be a clear understanding of the interaction between women's capital, field and habitus in water finance, prior to thinking about a reconstruction of the power relations in water governance, policy and management. The latter would enable the materiality of social conditions and positions within which women work and make sense of their lives to become managers in water finance.

Gurian and Annis (2008) propound a theory that explains gender disparity in water finance, also known as 'gender polarity'. It is well illustrated by the huge male-female gap in communication and in building relationships in business. In fact, women have enormous skills in persuading their clients, while men in general tend to communicate just to convey information, without necessarily building relationships. Since women are generally open to strangers and listen attentively to their clients without interruption, they are more likely than men to be used as entry points into water companies and institutions by new financiers, donors, investors and other corporate groups.[317] This can explain why the practice of water finance management has shifted from the traditional 3Ts (tax, tariffs and transfer) to more interactive 'public-private partnerships' involving more communication and trust than the traditional 'project return rates' and provision of collateral (e.g. in microfinance).

Finally, the fourth theory on women's leadership in water finance involves a clear understanding of their linguistic ability that compels 'behaviour change'. Burke (1966) says that the 'rhetor' uses 'terministic screens' to convey a certain agenda or idea that would appeal to a specific audience. Therefore, women leaders use language and images that direct the attention of men and women into feminist and romantic channels, rather than chauvinistic screens. Consequently, women leaders use a terminology that leads both men and women to a reflection on a specific figurative location that is safe and trustworthy (e.g. hoarding, banking or treasury safe) rather than to an unwanted place (e.g. stealing or bankruptcy). Baker and Start (1992)[318] strengthen this view by devoting attention to the art of persuasion. Women leaders tend to persuade their clients using stylistic identifications or acts of persuasion that cause the target audience to identify with trustworthiness, which is a must in the finance field. These women leaders establish rapport with financiers, donors, investors and other corporate leaders through identification of interests. In the same vein, they sentimentalize their leadership to attract both men and women. Therefore, the art of persuasion of women leaders in finance simply means identification and communication of the leadership interest to both men and women.

---

317  Hodgson and McCurdy, 2001; McQuiston and Morris, 2009
318  Baker and Start, 1992

## 6.3 Women's Role in Providing Strategic Financial Direction

Financing for water resource management has been a big challenge for most developing countries. The challenge can be attributed to the broad scope of WRM, which is not well defined and has no clear written strategy for its funding.[319] The need to improve the management of water resources is highlighted by the variability in the cost of water, the damage caused by water-related disasters, the effects of water on economic performance and concerns about protecting water-dependent environments.[320] The ultimate goal of WRM is to provide water security for a country. Water security has been described as 'the availability of an acceptable quantity and quality of water for health, livelihoods, ecosystems and production, coupled with an acceptable level of water-related risks to people, environments and economies'.[321] Water security, which underpins social and economic development, includes water governance, public stewardship and the provision of the infrastructure necessary for realizing the many services that water can offer.[322]

Achieving water security requires an efficient management of financial resources for investment in water infrastructure and development. This also involves a gender perspective in which the multiple uses of water in different ways by men and women are integrated in policy, planning, implementation, coordination and evaluation.[323] Yet, women's views in managing water resources are seldom incorporated in all the stages of community, regional and national development planning. They are only well known for providing water at the household level and for being custodians of water resources for agricultural use. But when it comes to sharing the benefits resulting from that water use, they are often left aside, or are simply 'kicked out' of management.[324] That is why they need to be empowered to take effective part in decision-making at all levels of WRM, including in finance.

Case studies confirm that in a number of countries (both OECD and non-OECD), water resources management fails to access the funds required to achieve policy objectives.[325] First of all, critical steps to mobilize adequate financing include estimating which costs need to be covered and how much financing is required to cover them. Studies show that financial gaps are a result of the failure of markets to recognize many of the benefits of WRM, so that there is a tendency to under-provide essential water-related services.[326] Secondly, the private and public benefits of water management can become blurred in some situations, making it difficult to identify clearly who benefits from the provision of services. Thirdly, beneficiaries of water-related services do not usually pay the full cost of such services or may 'freeload'; or conversely, potential private financiers may not benefit from the services, and so have reduced incentive to

---

319  EUWI, 2012.
320  EUWI, 2012, and CAP-NET, GWA 2006
321  Grey and Sadoff, 2007 cited in EUWI,2012
322  EUWI, 2012
323  OECD, 2016
324  Joshi and Fawcett, 2006
325  OECD, 2012
326  OECD, 2012

support them.[327] There is therefore a need for leadership that takes account of all the various aspects of WRM in a participatory manner, in order to increase funding for the water sector. Women leaders have been identified as having the knack of accepting information from all sides and not leaving anything to chance, hence positioning them as strategic leaders for financial management in water companies.[328]

The Kenyan expression *'Women do not leave anything to chance'* has been shown to be accurate by research into leadership styles. Women generally like to consider all aspects of a problem before they make a decision, and this trait fits them to be strategic managers. Research has shown that the skill most associated with strategic thinking is the proverbial ability to 'see around corners' – a skill that women possess.[329] Unfortunately, only a few women are found in managerial positions across the globe, even though they make up half of the human resources available to any country.[330] According to a report by the European Commission (2012),[331] as of the start of 2012, women held only 13.7% of board seats in the European Union. The trend in other parts of the world is the same. Although the figure in the US is slightly better (15.7%), Australia and Canada both see female board representation of only around 10%. India's boardrooms have less than 5% women. In 2010, women comprised only 6.5% of board members in the Asia-Pacific region, and in the Middle East and North Africa the figure was only 3.2%.[332] Greenberg notes that if a country's economic potential is not to suffer from the loss of half its human capacity, it is imperative to channel women's contributions into the economy by making them part of the decision-making processes.[333]

It has been noted that women in leadership score high on ego drive (persuasive motivation), assertiveness, empathy, urgency, flexibility and sociability. The strong people skills possessed by female leaders enable them to read situations accurately and to absorb information from all sides. This willingness to see all sides of a situation enhances their persuasive ability.[334]

> *They can zero in on someone's objections or concerns, weigh them appropriately, address them effectively and incorporate them into the grander scheme of things when appropriate. These female leaders are also able to bring others around to their point of view or alter their own point of view – depending upon the circumstances and information they uncover. They can do this because they genuinely understand and care about where others are coming from. This allows them to come at a subject from their audience's perspective, so that the people they are leading feel more understood, supported and valued.*[335]

---

327  OECD, 2012
328  Greenberg, 2005
329  Greenberg, 2005
330  Greenberg, 2005
331  EC, 2012
332  Corporate Women Directors International, 2010
333  Greenberg, 2005
334  Greenberg, 2005
335  Greenberg, 2005

Thus, these traits make women's contribution to the governance of WRM crucial. Globally women have been identified as controlling at least 64% of consumer spending and over 70% of household spending decisions, in some countries.[336] Thus, having women on the board gives corporations a competitive advantage in creating products and services that better meet their customers' needs. However, they have many unmet needs in finance, ranging from financial education and advice to actual funding they require at key inflexion points in their lives; hence the need for incorporating women in the financial management boards to improve on the pricing and fund collection processes.

Weaknesses in the execution of WRM in some water management areas account for the low rates of payment of WRM charges. The key lesson to be drawn from implementation of the WRM charge is the importance of engaging with customers in the process of setting the charges, and the need to demonstrate the benefits of the functions being charged for.[337] Recovery of investment in water services can be improved if the traditional roles of women and men in water management are recognized and promoted in an equitable manner.[338] Many studies have shown that women are very adept at empathy and collaboration and they need to be involved in decision-making with regard to financial management. They have been shown to have positive effects on corporate performance, as they do not allow the worst to happen. When given the chance, they can provide strategic direction to the financial management of water companies and institutions.[339]

Collecting money for WRM is more of an art than a science, and is governed by political pragmatism. Women are able to anticipate market shifts concerning customers, competitors, regulations, politics and the economy, and thus are well suited to occupy such strategic positions in water companies.[340] One of the most critical disciplines of a strategic leader is intellectual curiosity and acceptance of people who see the world differently. Women as strategic leaders could align the various divergent interests of the water sector in pursuit of the common goal of water resources management. They also understand how to engage with stakeholders and manage differences to create buy-in to new initiatives.[341]

Institutions that are run by managerial boards perform better when men and women sit together, rather than when they are run solely by men. The combination of female and male resources, knowledge, time and capabilities leads to greater effectiveness in policy implementation. There is greater efficiency in the management of these institutions, the development of their programmes and projects, and their use of finances and other resources such as water and wastewater.[342] Although funding for WRM

336 Silverstein and Sayre, 2009b cited in Patel, 2013; and Accenture, 2006 cited in Patel 2013
337 EUWI, 2012
338 CAP-NET and GWA, 2006
339 Greenberg, 2005; Barnakova, Shen and Krupp, 2015
340 Barnakova, Shen and Krupp, 2015
341 Barnakova, Shen and Krupp, 2015
342 IRC, 2004

has been a challenge, the same cannot be said of water and sanitation. The European Union Water Initiative (EUWI) notes that while little has been done on financing for WRM, progress has been made in improving the flow of finance for water supply and sanitation.[343] This could be attributed to the fact that most water and sanitation (WATSAN) committees have women on board at the decision-making level. In Ghana, for example, the WATSAN committees at the district level are made up of nine members, with both men and women.[344] Nonetheless, there is increasing recognition of the immense financial need for WRM across Africa and for the inclusion of women on the management boards. In Kenya, for instance, the constitutions of most water resources users' associations (WRUAs) provide for women to account for 50% of the management positions.[345] This has raised awareness of the key role of women as custodians of water resources, especially in male-dominant cultural settings.

The participation of women and men, young and old, rich and poor, in the use and management of infrastructure, in the choice of technologies, and in local maintenance, management and financing systems, leads in the longer run to greater sustainability and to the desired impact.[346] A comparative study of 88 community-managed water projects in 15 countries showed that those with greater and more equitable participation of women and men in planning and management performed significantly better in terms of effective functioning and access to all than did those with lower and/or less equitable levels of participation.[347]

Water infrastructure can be more widely and optimally used, maintained and sustained when the demands of women and men are considered, along with their expectations, experience, involvement and knowledge.[348] Such consideration enables targeted solutions in technology, payment and management systems, and other domains, and can result in better use of limited funds, human resources and water. There is thus a need for the different segments and layers in the water sector to be managed holistically, as deficiencies in any one layer caused by financing difficulties will have an impact on other water functions and services.[349] This can be done when women are given leadership positions.

## 6.4   Women's Role in Safeguarding the Treasury

Financial leaders have always been key to the successful running of any organization, and thus it is important to get the right person for such a position. Financial analysts agree generally that the skills and expertise of the finance officer or treasurer go beyond

---

343  EUWI, 2012
344  GWI, 2012
345  Alemu and Kidane, 2015
346  IRC, 2004
347  IRC, 2004
348  Schultz et al., 2007
349  CAP-NET, GWA 2006; EUWI, 2012

accounting, financial modelling and hard number skills.[350] Finding the right person to manage the treasury of water companies is very important, in order to ensure that water companies and institutions can mobilize money for the effective delivery of water and for the management of the water infrastructure.[351]

Finance officers must be close to the customer, so that they understand what drives wealth creation and where the money is made, and so plan ahead.[352] They should know the market trends and have an in-depth understanding of the business's opportunities, its competitors and customers.[353] Finance officers should be people centred, be able to build healthy relationships and be good communicators;[354] on top of all that, they should be able to take tough decisions, should the need arise. They have to grasp opportunities, and significantly they must have the courage to plan for growth, while ensuring that the accounting fundamentals are delivered.[355]

Thus, it emerges from the above that safeguarding the treasury is a task that needs to maintain a fine balance between control and creativity. In a 2010 survey of UK chief finance officers by the Directorbank group, only 8.5% of those polled were women.[356] Generally speaking, not many women rise to the high office of treasurer or finance director in businesses and water companies. But the few women who have made it have excelled compared to their male counterparts. The question is: What are the women finance officers doing right? 'Women have a great sense of ethical responsibility and the courage to stand up for what is right', says Accounting web (2009).[357]

Undoubtedly, women have what it takes to look after the treasury of water companies and institutions, if given the chance. The popular Ghanaian adage *'women are afraid of money'* underscores the great ethical responsibility that women exhibit in financial matters.[358] This means that monies given to women to handle are very well kept, since women are cautious about touching or using money that does not belong to them, for fear of being cast out by society if they are unable to repay it, should the need arise. Hence, most women shy away from debt and do not want to engage in activities that could burden them with debt. Women do not want to be associated with stealing or embezzlement of funds, unlike some of their male counterparts.[359]

Another convincing reason why women are good treasurers is that they exhibit less risky behaviour than is sometimes the case with men. This is because women perceive risk in a different way, and this calls forth different emotional reactions in them. Croson and Gneezy argue that the difference in the perception of risk is due to the difference in emo-

---

350  Messmer, 2006
351  CAP-NET, GWA 2006
352  Directorbank group, n.d.
353  WASREB, 2014.
354  Aaker, 1996
355  Directorbank group, n.d.
356  Directorbank group, n.d.
357  Accounting Web, 2009
358  Isidroand Sobral, 2015
359  Swamy et al., 2000

tional intensity – a stance that views risk as an emotion.[360] Moreover, when confronted with uncertainty, women report fear, whereas men report anger.[361] Accordingly, women are very careful when handling the finances of a company or a group. They are cautious about using the money or investing when they know that it is not their money, but is only being kept in trust. A case in point comes from Vietnam, where a union managed solely by women had great success in managing a sanitation revolving fund of USD 3 million. During the first phase of the project, the turnover generated by the women was more than double. This led to the project being scaled up in 2011, with Vietnam Bank for Social Policies (VBSP) extending USD 3.5 million in loans for water supply and sanitation, and USD 3.1 million being spent on the construction of facilities.[362]

Also, women are the primary users of water, not just in their reproductive role but also for productive purposes, to generate income. Those women who are not involved in agriculture (where water is needed for irrigation) are often engaged in cottage industries: local beer breweries, home restaurants, baking plants, shea processing plants, handicrafts, etc.[363] Thus, when it comes to knowing the customers (users of water), women have a great understanding of the markets and businesses that they engage with for water supply, and stay in tune with their customers.

Aside from maintaining their financial strength, water companies need to generate the energy and resources for growth. The creativity and control to ensure that this is achieved can be provided by women with marketing skills. Women who know the market and have a great sense of the different uses to which water is put can ensure that water pricing is done in an equitable manner, to mobilize more funds for the water companies. Studies have shown that women are noted for paying water charges, even though they have mobility restrictions and payment constraints.[364] Knowing all these categories of users will help better target water pricing for users.

## 6.5   Women's Roles in Running Revolving Funds

The provision of top-quality water in sufficient quantities has been a challenge for most water providers. The major issue surrounding the provision of water for multiple uses (as mentioned above) is budgetary constraints. Women's traditional role in organizing revolving funds can be put to use in WRM.[365]

Revolving funds have been a long-standing tradition among most African women affiliated to groups that offer a social network and mutual support.[366] These social networks are formed by women who come together because of some common interest

---

360   Croson and Gneezy, 2009
361   Grossman and Wood, 1993
362   EUWI-FWG, 2012
363   Sijbesma et al., 2008
364   CAP-NET, GWA 2006
365   Hulme and Mosley, 1996
366   Kosslyne, 2001

or because they have a similar challenge that they are seeking to address – more often than not, including the alleviation of poverty.[367] These groups are usually formed by women from the same homestead (same family or women who are married to men of the same descent) or community (the same village and religion; the same tribal lines or socio-economic status). They may work together as colleagues, friends or just neighbours.[368] The group formation is largely based on mutual understanding and most groups comprise 5-20 members.[369] Within development initiatives, women's groups may form around various issues related to livelihood and resources, such as water.[370] Thus, women in water users' associations, women in processing and women in the same community can employ revolving funds to raise money for the specific water service infrastructure that they want in their community, to help them in their reproductive and productive work. These women's groups might hold regular meetings to deliberate on the water issue or challenge, how much money they will need, and when and where they will make their contribution.

There are several ways of handling revolving funds. In Kenya, for instance, there are different types of women's social groups, each varying in operation and ideology. Some of these groups are of the merry-go-round type; some are peer-to-peer banking and lending groups; and some are property acquisition groups.

*Merry-go-round women's groups:*[371] In 'merry-go-round' groups in Kenya, women's meetings may be regular or else linked to seasonal cash-flow cycles in rural communities. Each member contributes the same amount at each meeting, and one member takes the whole sum once. As a result, each member is able to access a larger sum of money during the cycle, and use it for whatever purpose she wishes. This method of saving is a popular alternative to the risks of saving at home, where family and relatives may demand access to the money. The lump sum is used to purchase household items, pay school fees or invest in business, including selling water.[372]

When Kenyan water services were decentralized in 2014, some members of the women's groups took the opportunity to open up water kiosks at strategic places in the slum areas as selling points. They sell a 20 litre jerry-can of water for 5 Kenyan shillings (KES). It was noted that water vendors make more profit than hawkers, and with less risk.[373]

*Peer-to-peer banking and lending women's groups:*[374] In this type of group, women agree to meet for a definite period in order to save and borrow together. This concept is more common at the workplace. Women pool their resources by contributing a certain sum of money (also known as a 'share') every month for one year. Each individual member contributes money to the value of one or more 'shares', depending on her

367  KWFT, 2011
368  Morduch, 1999
369  Morduch, 1999
370  Morduch, 1999
371  Yunus, 2007
372  Robinson, 2001
373  Cherunya, Janezic and Leuchner, 2015
374  Lewa, 2002

financial position. The amount she can borrow depends on how many 'shares' she will have contributed at the end of the year. Occasionally, a member may be loaned three times the total amount that she is expected to have contributed by the end of one year.

*Property acquisition women's groups:*[375] In this type of group, women come together to purchase items and/or to acquire property. For instance, women may form a group with the main aim of furnishing their houses, each in turn. A group with such a function is mostly joined by women who are newly married or who want to increase or improve the quality of the items in the household. Once the group is formed, women discuss the items they need to purchase. Then they draw up a list indicating the quantity and quality of the desired items. The list is debated and the sequence of items to be bought is agreed. Generally, the list starts with the most desired items. Household items may range from furniture to foodstuffs (flour and sugar), bedding and cutlery. Women buy these items in bulk from wholesale dealers more cheaply than they can buy them from retail shops.[376] The same techniques for mobilizing funds used by the women of Kenya can be adopted to mobilize funds for WRM at the community level. Microfinance institutions have utilized this concept to disburse funds, train women and empower women in the water industry.[377]

Makato has related how a women's group known as 'Utawala' in Nairobi's Kibera slum used the money it got from their savings with a microfinance institution to start a water business.[378] The women's group received a cheque for KES 50,000 (that is about USD 500) and immediately used the money to acquire a machine that makes chlorine for treating water. The machine was acquired for KES 25,000 (equivalent of USD 250). They then applied for and received a licence from the Nairobi County Council; and they bought containers from an industrial area. They now treat the piped water and sell it in bottles of 500 ml and 300 ml. The area's residents buy the bottles of water for KES 30 and KES 20, respectively, and the water is also supplied to local mini-supermarkets. The Utawala women's group has a dream of becoming a major producer of clean drinking water and in this way of saving the community from the waterborne diseases that are rife in the region. Apart from treating water, they also sell the extra chlorine they produce to residents at subsidized prices, so that they can treat the drinking water at home. The case presented by these Kenyan women's groups is quite compelling. If adopted to finance water companies and institutions, the revolving fund system could not only help water managers to provide infrastructure, but could also enable the community to get involved in setting up water businesses.[379]

---

375 Lewa, 2002
376 Knowthis.com, 2016
377 GWP, 2005
378 Makato, 2015
379 Littefield et al., 2003

## 6.6    Women's Role in Marketing Management

Women trade in everything they come across. In most African communities, the art of trading or sales has been the major preoccupation of women. Several studies show that right from rural to urban centres, informal to formal employment, women engage in sales and petty trading.[380] They sell everything – from farm produce to provisions and clothing. In addition to her farming or occupation, almost every woman engages in petty trading to top up her income. In Ghana, for example, women are in control of the buying and marketing of farm produce. After the harvest, the men give the produce to their wives to sell. Women have such great skill in selling that most sales companies find it prudent to have women as sales executives, so that they meet their sales targets.[381]

The sales profession is based on communication: the sales professionals persuade their clients to purchase a product or service. The ability to convince a buyer to buy your products is key in marketing, and women have enormous skill in talking and per-suading clients. According to Gurian and Annis, women love to talk about themselves, which often leads them to reveal and relate more about the product they are selling than men do.[382] Men, in general, tend to communicate in order to convey information; women typically communicate to build relationships. Women tend to include more pleasant endings, such as 'Have a nice day!'. They use lots of questions, and they use upward inflection, turning statements into questions: 'It's a nice day, isn't it?' Men tend to ask fewer questions in order to stimulate conversation with customers. They tend to end sentences more abruptly and also to avoid upward inflection. Though open to strangers, women are more likely than men to use tentative language.[383] McQuiston and Morris reinforce this point by noting that women are more likely to employ hed-ges, qualifiers, disclaimers, tag questions and intensifiers, such as 'very' or 'really' when selling a product, and they listen attentively to the client without interruption.[384] Men tend to interrupt, use more direct language, and may become frustrated when female colleagues 'meander' during a discussion.[385]

Female salespeople are more likely than males to build a relationship with the client before starting the sales process. Male salespeople tend to build a relationship *during* the sales process. Men tend to speak louder than women, which may be off-putting for female clients. Male salespeople often focus more on data and use fewer emotional tactics when making a sale. Women are more likely to rely on relationship skills and emotions to close a deal.[386] These female characteristics distinguish women from their male counterparts, leading them to excel in sales and marketing.

---

380  Getu and Mulinge, 2013; and Otoo, 2012
381  Hunter, 2014
382  Gurian and Annis, 2008
383  Getu and Mulinge, 2013
384  McQuiston and Morris, 2009
385  Leaper, and Robnett. 2011
386  Getu and Mulinge, 2013

A study by Franke and Park (2006) that sought to explain why it is that women make such good salespeople correlated antecedents and consequences of adaptive selling behaviour (ASB) and customer orientation (CO) and revealed that ASB increases self-rated, manager-rated and objective measures of performance, whereas CO increases only self-rated performance based on the salesperson gender and selling experience.[387] Both ASB and CO increase job satisfaction. Tests of reciprocal relationships indicate that ASB increases CO, and job satisfaction increases performance, rather than vice versa. Selling experience increases performance, but not job satisfaction; and saleswomen rate their performance and satisfaction slightly higher than do salesmen. The magnitudes of the relationships indicate that ASB and selling experience have a greater effect than CO and gender on salesperson performance.

As the primary users of water for both domestic and commercial activities, women are well suited to marketing the image of water for companies. As may be seen from the preceding paragraphs, getting more women involved in water marketing is likely to increase sales and profits for these companies.

## 6.7    Women's Role in Spearheading Communication and Engagement

Communication can be seen as the foundation of modern organizations and lies at the core of competency for the success or failure of an organization. Communication, when properly executed, connects every member of a project or an organization to a common set of strategies, goals and actions. For better outcomes, these components must be effectively shared by leaders and understood by all stakeholders.[388]

> Communication does not just focus on content (e.g. the accurate exchange of information or adequacy of conveying the intended meaning) but on the larger context of communication. It focuses on nonverbal cues as well as verbal content. It also looks at the relational context between the sender and receiver within the larger social, organizational and cultural context. [389]

Communication in water companies is very important not just for sales, but for a proper and good image of the company. People's patronage of the water that is supplied by a company depends largely on the extent of their confidence in the company. Consumers' knowledge of the product is derived from information gathered through proper imaging of the organization through a proper communication strategy employed by the organization. The success of a company's communications depends not only on its external communications, but also on its internal communication.[390]

---

387   Franke and Park (2006)
388   Baker, 2002; and PMI, 2013
389   Baker, 2002
390   PMI, 2013

Communication is one of the most difficult skills to master, and is probably a great source of friction and problems in any organization. Situation, time, culture and customs, and gender styles affect and complicate the process.[391] It is identified as the most critical leadership skill, as it involves the ability to listen, read body language, ask questions, provide feedback and generate effective two-way communication. It builds trust that can prevent performance problems down the road. Communication also demands the ability to comfortably use a variety of communication styles, in order to articulate goals and objectives that pave the way for healthy working relationships within an organization. Providing relevant information allows employees to participate fully in their work and leads to better outcomes.[392]

In the Kenyan and Ghanaian societies, men and women communicate differently: the styles that they use have been described as 'debate vs. relate', 'report vs. rapport', or 'competitive vs. cooperative'. Men often look for straightforward solutions to problems and seek advice that is useful, whereas women tend to try and establish intimacy by discussing problems and showing concern and empathy, in order to reinforce relationships.[393]

Women are sensitive to context, good at picking up information that is incidental to a task that is set them, and are readily distracted. Female managers are seen by both male and female subordinates as better communicators than male managers. They have superior verbal skills.[394] In this vein, Christine Gorman asks the question 'Are women innately better at reading words and understanding emotions or do they just get more practice?' and implies that hormones may be involved.[395] Nicholas Wade agrees, relating that women's innate skills may give them an edge in perceptual speed, verbal fluency and communication skills. There appears to be a genetic connection to these skills, and many seem to imply abilities akin to what has been termed 'women's intuition'. Intuition plays an important role in the communication process with women and serves a valuable purpose, so much so that current leaders in the world of business recommend learning to trust one's senses and intuition.[396] Women thus make a good case for being engaged in spearheading communication in water companies, so as to bring the desired impact in promoting the image of water companies for maximum profit.

---

391  Kelly, 1997
392  Blanchard, 2006
393  Kelly, 1997
394  Kelly, 1997
395  Kelly, 1997
396  Mohindra and Azhar, 2012

# References

Aaker, D. 1996. Building strong brands. New York, NY: Simon and Schuster.

Accountingweb. 2009. Success secrets of women who have risen to CFO in major companies. Available at: http://www.accountingweb.com/aa/auditing/success-secrets-of-women-who-have-risen-to-cfo-in-major-companies (Accessed on 12.03.2010)

African Ministers' Council on Water (AMCOW). 2012. Status Report on the Application of Integrated Approaches to Water Resources Management in Africa.

Alemu, B. and Kidane, D. 2015. Rainwater harvesting: An optiuon for dry land agriculture in the arid and semi-arid Ethiopia. Int. J. Water Res. Eng. Vol. 7(2): 17-28.

Ansoff, I. 1990. Implanting Strategic Management, Second Edition. Englewoods Cliffs, NJ: Prentice-Hall.

Baker, A. K. 2002. Organizational Communication. Available at: http://www.au.af.mil/au/awc/awcgate/doe/benchmark/ch13.pdf (Accessed on 12.03.2010).

Baker, M.J. and Start, S. 1992. Marketing and Competitive Success. London: Philip Allen.

Barnakova, Y., Shen, F. and Krupp, S. 2015. Women as Strategic Leaders: The Need and the Critical Skills. MWorldVol. 13 Issue 4.

Biel, A., and Thogersen, J. 2007. Activation of social norms in social dilemmas: A review of the evidence and reflections on the implications for environmental behavior. Journal of Economic Psychology, 28, 93–112.

Blanchard, K. 2006. Critical Leadership Skill. Available at: http://www.kenblanchard.com/img/pub/pdf_critical_leadership_skills.pdfs (Accessed on 12.03.2010).

Bourdieu, P. 1992. The logic of practice. Cambridge, MA: Harvard University Press. (Original work published in 1980)

Burke, K. 1966. Language as symbolic action. Assays on life, literature and methods. Los Angeles, CA: University of California Berkeley.

CAP-NETand GWA. 2006. Why Gender Matters: a tutorial for water managers. CAP-NET International network for Capacity Building in Integrated Water Resources Management, Delft.

Cherunya, P.C., Janezic, C. and Leuchner, M. 2015. Sustainable supply of safe drinking water for underserved households in Kenya: Investigating the Viability of Decentralized Solutions. Water , 7(10): 5437- 5457

Cleaver, F. 1998. Choice, Complexity and Change: Gendered livelihoods and the management of water. Agricultural human values 15:293-299. Dordrecht: Kluwer Academic Publishers.

Connell, R.W. 2005. Masculinities. (2nd ed). California: University of California Press.

Connell, R.W. 2002. Gender: Short introductions. Cambridge, MA: Polity Press.

Croson, R. and Gneezy, U. 2009. Gender difference in preferences. Journal of Economic Literature 47 (2), 448–474.

Directorbank Group. (n.d.). What makes an outstanding finance director?

Doyle, P. . 1992. What are the excellent companies? Journal of Mktg Mgt, 8 (2): 25-31.

EUWI. 2012. Financing of water resources management. Experiences from sub-Saharan Africa. Stockholm: EUWIand GWP.

EUWI – Finance Working Group (FWG) . 2012. Small-scale finance for water and sanitation. Stockholm: EUWI.

Franke G. R. and Park, J. 2006. Salesperson Adaptive Selling Behavior and Customer Orientation: A Meta-Analysis Journal of Marketing Research 693 Vol. 43 (693): 693–702.

Global Water Initiative, Ghana. 2012. Report of Research on the Sustainability of Community WATSAN Committee's Operations and Maintenance Capacity of Water Facilities. Available at: http://www.gwiwestafrica.org/sites/default/files/28_gh42_report_on_sustainability_of_community_watsan_in_ghana_1.pdf (Accessed on 06.03.2016).

Global Water Partnership (GWP). 2005. Integrated Water Resources Management Toolbox. Available at: www.gwptoolbox.org (Accessed on 13.05.2007)

Greenberg, H. 2005. The Qualities That Distinguish Women Leaders. Available at: http://www.albany.edu/womeningov/programs/fwpp/reading02.pdf (Accessed on 12.03.2010).

Gurian, M and Annis, B. 2008. Leadership and the Sexes: Using Gender Science to Create Success in Business. Hoboken, NJ: John Wiley Sons Inc.

Haraway, D. 1990.'Reading Buchi Emecheta: Contests for Women's Experience in Women's Studies,' Inscriptions 3/4 (1988): 107-24. Revised for: Women: a Cultural Review 1, no. 3: 240-55.

Hodgson, D.L. and McCurdy, S. 2001. 'Wicked' Women and the Reconfiguration of Gender in Africa. Portsmouth, N.H.: Heinemann.

Hulme, D. and Mosley,P. 1996. Finance against poverty. Vols 1 &2. London: Routledge.

Hunter, M. 2014. 'The Sales Hunter-Eyes on Sales.' Sales Motivation Blog. Available at: http://www.eyesonsales.com/author/the_sales_hunter/ (Accessed on 06.03.2016).

IRC [International Water and Sanitation Centre]. 2004. Gender and Water. Available at: http://www.gewamed.net/share/img_documents/11_back_soec1.pdf (Accessed on 12.03.2010).

Joshi, D. and Fawcett, B. 2006. Water projects and women's empowerment. Available at: https://assets.publishing.service.gov.uk/media/57a08d67ed915d3cfd0019f6/R65752.pdf (Accessed on 13.07.2010).

Kelley, M.J.M. 1997. Gender Differences and Leadership A Study. Available at: http://www.au.af.mil/au/awc/awcgate/awc/97-104.pdf (Accessed on 09.11.2000).

Knowthis.com. 2016. Benefits of wholesalers. Wholesaling tutorials. Available at: http://www.Knowthis.com/bbenefits-of-wholesalers (Accessed on 24.10.2016).

Kotler, P. 1991. Marketing Management: Analysis, Planning and Control, 8th Edition. Englewoods Cliffs, NJ: Prentice-Hall.

KWFT. 2011. Kenya Women Finance Trust (DTM) Report 2010. Nairobi: KWFT.

Kosslyne, S. 2001. Psychology. Needham Heights, MA: Allynand Bacon.

Leaper, C. and Robnett, R.D. 2011. Women are more likely than men to use tentative language, aren't they? A meta-analysis testing for gender differences and moderators. Psychology of Women Quarterly, 35(1): 129-142.

Lewa, R. M. 2002. Capacity building programs (CBPs) among women groups in Mombasa district Kenya. M.A thesis. Nairobi: University of Nairobi

Littefield,E., Morduch, J. and Hashemi, S. 2003. Is Microfinance an Effective Strategy to Reach the Millennium Development Goal? Washington, DC.: Consultative Group to Assist the Poor (CGAP).

Martinsen, C. 2008: Social marketing in sanitation- More than selling toilets. Stockholm Water Front, No1, April 2008: 14-16.

McQuiston, D. H. and Morris, K. A. 2009. Gender Differences in Communication: Implications for Salespeople. Scholarship and Professional Work - Business. Paper 45. Available at: http://digitalcommons.butler.edu/cob_papers/45 (12.03.2010).

Makato, S. 2015. it's mixed bag for Uwezo Fund in Mukuru kwa Njenga: Daily nation March 25, 2015. Nairobi: Nation Media House.

Messmer, M. 2006. 10 Qualities of Successful Financial Executives. Available at: http://www.imanet.org/docs/default-source/sf/6careers-pdf.pdf?sfvrsn=0 (12.03.2010).

Mohindra, V. and Azhar, S. 2012. Gender Communication: A Comparative Analysis of Communicational Approaches of Men and Women at Workplaces. Journal of Humanities and Social Science (JHSS) Volume 2, Issue 1, PP 18-27.

Morduch, J. 1999. The Micro Finance Promise, Journal of Economic Literature. Vol. 37 ( 4): 1569 -1614.

Morrell, R., Epstein, D., Unterhalter, E., Bhana, D. and Moletsane, R. 2009. Towards gender equality: South African schools during the HIV and AIDS epidemic. Scottsville: University of KwaZulu-Natal Press.

Mullen, B. and Johnson, C. 1990. Distinctiveness-based illusory correlations and stereotyping: A meta-analytic integration. British Journal of Social Psychology, Vol. 29 (1): 11–28.

Mulinge, M.M. and Getu, M. 2013. Impacts of Climate Change and Variability on Pastoralist Women in Sub- Saharan Africa. Organisation for social science research in eastern and southern Africa. Kampala: Fountain Publishers Ltd

OECD [Organisation for Economic Co-operation and Development].2012. Studies on Water a Framework for Financing Water Resources Management. Marseille: OECD.

OECD [Organisation for Economic Co-operation and Development]. 2016. Condition for success 1 'Good governance': The Synthesis Report of Target 1 Stakeholders' Engagement for Effective Condition for success 1 'Good governance': The Synthesis Report of Target 1 Stakeholders' Engagement for Effective Water Policy and Management. In Proceedings of the 6th World Water Forum, Marseille, France, 12–17 March 2012. Available online:

http://www.worldwaterforum6.org/uploads/tx_amswwf/CS1.1__Stakeholder__s_engagement_for_effective_water_policy_and_management_Report.pdf (accessed on 09 November 2016).

Otoo, B.J. 2012. Micro-Credit for Micro-Enterprise: A Study of Women 'Petty' Traders in Central Region, Ghana. International Journal of Scientific Research in Education, Vol. 5(3), 247-259.

Project management Institute, 2013. The High Cost of Low Performance: The Essential Role of Communications. Available at: http://www.pmi.org/~/media/PDF/Business-Solutions/The-High-Cost-Low-Performance-The-Essential-Role-of-Communications.ashx (Accessed on 24.10.2016).

Robinson, M. 2001.The microfinance revolution: sustainable finance for the poor. Washington, DC: The World Bank.

Schultz et al., P.W., Nolan, J.M., Cialdini, R.B., Goldstein, N.J., and Griskevicius, V. 2007. The constructive, destructive, and reconstructive power of social norms. Psychological Science, 18: 429– 434.

Sijbesma,C., Verhagena,J., Nanavaty, R. and James ,A. J. 2008. Impacts of domestic water supply on gender and income: results from a participatory study in a drought-prone region in Gujarat, India. London: IWA Publishing.

Solanes, M. and Gonzalez-Villarreal, F. 1999.The Dublin Principles for Water as Reflected in a Comparative Assessment of Institutional and Legal Arrangements for Integrated Water Resources Management. Stockholm: Global Water Partnership (GWP) and Swedish International Development Agency (SIDA).

WASREB [Water Services Regulatory Board]. 2014. Assessing options to achieve commercial viability and financial sustainability of water supply and sanitation services. Nairobi: German Cooperation (GiZ).

WRMA. 2010. Enforcement of Water Use Charges and Water Quality Thresholds in Kenya. WRMA Training Workshop Manual. Meru: WRMA.

UNEP.1997. The Fair Share Water Strategy for Sustainable Development in Africa. Nairobi: UNEP.

Webb, J., Schirato, T. and Danaher, G. 2002. Understanding Bourdieu. London: Sage Publications.

Yunus, M.2007. Creating a world without poverty: Social business and the future of capitalism. New York, NY: Public Affairs Publishers.

# Index

This is the first volume of three in the series on *Innovative Water Finance in Africa*. You can find these and many more of our titles online for Open Access. Please visit our website, www.nai.uu.se, for free downloads and more information.

⊙ OPEN ACCESS The Nordic Africa Institute (Nordiska Afrikainstitutet) is a centre for research, knowledge, policy advice and information on Africa. Based in Uppsala, Sweden, we are a government agency, funded jointly by Sweden, Finland and Iceland. We believe in promoting open-access dissemination of research findings and scientific knowledge. We believe that open access benefits researchers, policy-makers and society in general.

Nordiska Afrikainstitutet
The Nordic Africa Institute

ISBN 9789171068156
9 789171 068156

www.ingramcontent.com/pod-product-compliance
Lightning Source LLC
Chambersburg PA
CBHW060803270326
41926CB00003B/76